The Deep State:

15 Surprising Dangers You Should Know

The Deep State:
15 Surprising Dangers You Should Know

Craig A. Huey

Media Specialists

The Deep State: 15 Surprising Dangers You Should Know
Copyright © 2018 by Craig Huey
All rights reserved

Media Specialists, 21171 S. Western Ave., Suite 260 Torrance, CA 90501, USA

ISBN: 978-0-359-16859-0

My wife, Shelly, is an inspiration in declaring truth with love.

I'm so grateful to the Lord for giving me such an incredible gift. Thank you Shelly, for listening and encouraging.

And to my kids – Asher, Julia, Caleb, Kelly and Cory – who have helped me see clearly the danger that lies in our future if the Deep State is not exposed and destroyed.

And a special thanks to Kelsey Yarnell, who has taken my ideas, research and experiences and helped put them into a coherent exposé of the Deep State and what can be done to drain the swamp.

Plus, thank you to Kent Barry for his powerful editing, critiquing and insight.

Finally, I praise God for giving me an understanding of reality, the word of God for understanding objective truth in the age of relativism. And Jesus Christ, for salvation, joy, love, peace … and hope, despite impossible circumstances.

Table of Contents

Introduction ix

Chapter 1: What is the Deep State? 1

Chapter 2: Deep State Under the Radar Power:
Government Employees 15

Chapter 3: Government Agencies: Politicized and Transformed
Into Deep State Strongholds of Influence and Power 27

Chapter 4: The Bloated Bureaucracy: Fat Paychecks,
Socialist Ideology, Waste and Inefficiency 45

Chapter 5: The Disturbing Weaponization of U.S.
Intelligence Agencies: The Deep State in the FBI, CIA and More 61

Chapter 6: Warning: Judicial Activists are Legislating
a Dangerous Far-Left Ideology From the Bench 77

Chapter 7: K Street and the Lobbyists:
The Invisible Deep State Support Network 91

Chapter 8: Establishment Republicans:
Uneasy Deep State Allies Betraying Basic Principles 105

Chapter 9: Unseen, Unknown, Unaccountable! The Unholy
Alliance Between the Deep State and Nonprofit Groups 115

Chapter 10: The Deep State's Dirty Little Secret:
Organizing for Action (OFA) 129

Chapter 11: Voter Fraud: Earning the Deep State More Votes,
More Power...While Trampling on Your Rights and Suppressing
Your Voice as a Citizen 143

Chapter 12: The Media: Giving Voice to the Deep State 157

Chapter 13: 12 Examples of the Deep State's War on Christianity 175

Chapter 14: The False Hope: Eight Reasons
the Deep State Bureaucracy Cannot Be Fixed 197

Chapter 15: The Deep State: The Road to Socialism! 211

Epilogue: We Must Fight the Deep State 219

Footnotes 231

Additional Sources 247

Foreword

The election of President Donald Trump unleashed an historic attack from those opposed to any change that would endanger existing government programs and the bureaucracy.

The Deep State fought back against draining the swamp, downsizing government agencies and calling out the ineffectiveness of the great, vast bureaucracy in Washington, D.C.

For the first time, Americans saw a glimpse of the corruption, unfairness, unequal treatment, favoritism and much more in our nation's government agencies.

For the first time, abuses of power – which exist at all levels of government – have been exposed.

Rightfully, much of the focus has been on the intelligence agencies, specifically the Department of Justice and the FBI.

But the manipulation, control and sabotage revealed in the intelligence agencies are much deeper and more profound than anyone has imagined.

You'll soon discover the disturbing reality of Deep State corruption and abuse of power throughout the federal government, as well as in state and local governments.

You will also learn about Deep State supporters who are often unseen and unnoticed, but yet powerful influences in the transformation of our culture and politics.

The following pages expose the reality, causes and solutions to the Deep State. And, they give direction to eliminating the Deep State's power, influence and abuse.

CHAPTER 1
What is the Deep State?

The Deep State: Fact or fiction?

The liberal media would like you to think that the Deep State isn't real.

They would like you to think that it's a fairy tale created by Conservatives or Libertarians — a myth promoted by President Trump, Steve Bannon and Fox.

News stations, magazines, newspapers, online publications, social media and Hollywood push one idea: Anyone who believes the Deep State is real is crazy.

I have personally received insulting, enraged emails, postal mail, tweets and Facebook messages after I have spoken to groups or appeared on radio or TV to talk about the Deep State.

Take a look at the following headline, written for an article in the liberal publication, *The New Yorker*:

THERE IS NO DEEP STATE

Here's the truth:

The New Yorker is sympathetic to big government, bureaucracy and the Deep State. So, it denies the Deep State's existence.

But the Deep State *does* exist.

The Deep State is a massive decentralized network of progressive ideologues operating at all levels of the federal government. These ideologues include career government bureaucrats, elected members of the legislative branch, appointed judges in the judicial branch and appointed heads of the federal agencies in the executive branch, the intelligence agencies and the military.

But the Deep State is much more than a political or governmental phenomenon.

It also permeates the mainstream news media, social media, public education, the Hollywood film industry and more....

And it lives to:

1. Grow bigger.
2. Maintain power and influence.
3. Advance a progressive, anti-God ideology in every part of society.
4. Resist and attack anyone who disagrees.

For more than 20 years, I have watched the Deep State take hold of our culture and politics in America.

I have researched how this big-government ideology has seized social and political power and authority at the expense of individual freedom, the founding principles of our democratic republic and the well-being of our nation.

I have also been a business owner for more than 40 years — and I have seen the difference between a private bureaucracy that develops within a company and a government bureaucracy, which is at the core of the Deep State.

I've seen the Deep State dramatically influence all levels of government.

The Deep State has been facilitated by:

– The growth of big government

– The creep of the administrative state

- The politicization of the American media
- Radically liberal politics being promoted in universities and other American institutions
- Increasing pressure and hostility aimed at Conservative and Judeo-Christian values
- The intentional silencing of dissenting voices

The power of the state — the government — demands obedience and leads to the trampling of individual rights and freedom.

Now, Trump's presidency has caused the Deep State to rear its ugly head like never before, going from being quiet and hidden to hysterical and obvious.

His policies and boldness in calling out the Deep State have made it impossible for dangerous Deep State ideologues to hide. Their corruption, lies and manipulation are out in the open for everyone to see — and they're angry.

In the following chapters, you'll "discover" the Deep State, and where it exists. Don't be surprised if you begin to notice its ugly and pervasive influence where you may never have expected it.

You'll begin to see:

.... How the Deep State has abused its power to promote its own political agenda

.... How it affects you and your family

.... And how to fight back.

Who is the Deep State?

The Deep State exists in both the public and private sector, in the Democratic and Republican parties. It's not partisan; it's ideological.

The Deep State is not unique to the 21st century. What's different today is that Deep State-aligned ideologues want to advance their value system through every sector of society. And, they will fiercely resist anyone who disagrees.

Today, ideological warfare to transform the government, media, legislative decisions and culture has become a reality — and a nightmare.

The Deep State's power over you and your family produces:

- Repeated attacks on individual liberties
- Breaches of government security
- Trampling of constitutional rights
- Indoctrination and false news spread through the media and globalist propaganda.

The Deep State works in both the government and the private sector to influence every area of our lives and exercise control over all Americans.

The Deep State in the Government

The Deep State exists in all branches of the government, including the executive branch, Congress, the judiciary and the vast, unelected bureaucracy.

The Deep State is primarily a decentralized network of government employees that is effectively working to:

- Undermine the legitimacy and authority of President Trump

- Stop progress and change that negatively affects a bureaucracy

- Hinder the individual liberties of Americans like you

- Promote an ideology of big government, increased regulations, higher taxes and state socialism
- And protect itself from transparency, accountability and change

The Deep State: The Obama Appointees

Many of the Deep State operatives are appointees from the Obama administration.

The Obama appointees were selected based on their support for a radical progressive ideology. And they were ordered to support or oppose policies tied to their socialist beliefs.

Obama strategically appointed young people who have little or no experience in business or management. But, they are passionate about promoting socialism over free enterprise throughout the government.

Their god is the State; Their religion is collectivism. Their objective is transforming our culture and politics into a socialist government and economy.

I have been to Washington, D.C. many times since the Reagan administration in the 1980s. But since 2009, there has been a big difference.

From the beginning of the Obama administration to the Trump administration, I have met many progressive and socialist movers and shakers and decision-makers in D.C. I've seen young, aggressive, ideologically-driven bureaucrats first-hand in restaurants, in parks and in meetings. They are promoters of larger government and socialism, influencing policy and directing the government agencies of the United States.

The predominant culture in Washington, D.C.,

is like a post-graduate school of young millennials. Individuals in their 20s or early 30s dominate. Many were handpicked by Obama, based on their support for a radical leftist ideology. They came aboard supporting Obama's policies, and now they are bitter because they no longer have the control and influence they once had.

Many Obama holdovers are entrenched in their hard-left beliefs. They are resistant to change and committed to promoting their own agenda. And they are determined to maintain their inefficient and dysfunctional bureaucratic ways, and to transform our society based on their socialist worldview.

But Deep State ideology is not exclusively promoted by Obama appointees. The Deep State is also being advanced by holdovers from the Bush and Clinton administrations.

In the following pages of this book, you will learn more about how Deep State-influenced government employees advance their dangerous ideology.

The Deep State: Administrative Bureaucracy

You'll see how the Deep State exists in the massive administrative state, which spends $66 million every hour to fund fat paychecks for an inefficient, wasteful bureaucracy.[1] Bureaucratic agents openly admit that they resist and ignore executive orders they don't agree with, and they work hard to maintain their power.

The Deep State: Corruption of the Intelligence Agencies

You will also see how the Deep State has become entrenched in America's intelligence agencies.

The FBI, CIA and NSA have been transformed into bastions of Deep State influence. These agencies have been politically weaponized by this dangerous ideology. They have abused their power again and again to advance a political agenda. And their actions have done great harm to U.S. national security in an unprecedented abuse of power.

The Deep State: Judges Legislating from the Bench

You'll discover that the Deep State is promoted by judicial activists who legislate from the bench. These are judges who do not interpret the law according to the Constitution. Instead, they advance their own twisted ideology by imposing biased and politicized fiats from the bench.

You'll be shocked at the far-reaching and pervasive influence of the Deep State in every part of the government. The Deep State threatens our individual freedom…mocks our beliefs … attempts to ambush positive change … and rails against any hint of our nation's traditional values.

Government is the major problem. But it doesn't end there.

The Deep State in the Private Sector

The Deep State has extensive roots and a massive reach that go beyond the government. It is forcefully expanding through:

- Lobbyists and K street power brokers, who use their influence and money to manipulate policy
- Massive nonprofits, supporting the Deep State

and transferring funds to radical, anti-business, far-left groups for political action

- Social media and major internet platforms, which unfairly censor anyone with a belief system that differs from Deep State ideology

The Deep State is rooted in corrupt strongholds of power throughout our sociopolitical system and our culture. The Deep State deliberately manipulates what you see on your laptops, your smart phone, your television and in movie theaters.

In later chapters of this book, you'll see how the Deep State has influenced the economy, the legal system, elections and even your children.

RESIST

One of the primary aims of the Deep State is to resist anyone who disagrees with their radical leftist ideological viewpoint.

This is what you need to be aware of — something few people know about or understand.

The Deep State has picked up the slogan of "resist." Resist change, resist progress, resist the opinions and actions of anything that threatens or reverses the growth and expansion of the State ... and its power-hungry bureaucracy.

It's a guise for control and manipulation, and it must be stopped.

In the following chapters, you'll dive deeper into the sordid truths behind each Deep State entity. You'll discover how Deep State operatives manipulate opinion and abuse power at the expense of the American people.

You'll also find out what you can do about it.

But in order to really understand the Deep State, you'll have to go back to its roots, which can be traced all the way back to early 20th-century Turkey.

The Seeds of the Deep State in Turkey

Many people are surprised to learn that the seeds of what is known today as the "Deep State" are rooted in Turkey – a country that continues to be rocked by social and political upheaval.

Derin devlet is a Turkish term meaning "deep state." It alludes to a "shadow government" — an unofficial and covert system of authority that exists alongside the recognized government.

The *derin devlet* has had a huge influence on the history of Turkey beginning in the decades that preceded its founding as the Republic of Turkey, in 1923 — and it continues to wield great power over its 80 million people.

Early in the 20th century, the country we know today as Turkey was the major power at the center of the Ottoman Empire, a massive domain that spread across the Middle East and parts of Europe and North Africa.

But political chaos and its devastating involvement in World War I weakened the Ottoman Empire, leaving it vulnerable to change in its political leadership.

In 1908, the beginning of modern Turkey was set in motion by the formation of a political faction known as the Committee of Union and Progress (CUP). Also known as the "Young Turks," this group of intellectuals, bureaucrats, army officers and students was opposed to the absolute rule of Sultan Abdül Hamid II and led a rebellion against him.

Ultimately, the Young Turks were successful in their efforts. They eventually toppled the Ottoman Empire and declared the Republic of Turkey, led by "Young Turk" and military hero Mustafa Kemal (named "Atatürk" or "Father of the Turks" by the Turkish Grand National Assembly), who became its first president.

In the century that followed, the *derin devlet* has variously sought to undermine or protect (depending on the interests of the permanent bureaucracy) the central government by any means possible: including thuggery, criminal acts and all forms of corruption.

And they continued to commission underground operatives to "maintain" the interests of the state, regardless of who ran the country.

It has supported ongoing collusion between Turkey's powerful military and its successive governments, including during multiple military coup d'états, with paramilitary forces and even drug traffickers and violent gangs playing a destabilizing role in the nation's most turbulent periods.

The *derin devlet* has been described as a "presumed clandestine network" of Turkish "military officers and their civilian allies" who, for decades, "suppressed and sometimes murdered dissidents, Communists, reporters, Islamists, Christian missionaries, and members of minority groups — anyone thought to pose a threat to the secular order."[2]

Oxford scholar and Tufts Professor of History Hugh Roberts has called it "the 'shady nexus' between the police and intelligence services, 'certain politicians and organized crime,' whose members believe they are authorized 'to get up to all sorts of unavowable things' because they are 'custodians of the higher interests of the nation.'"[3]

Today, though radical Islamist President Recep Tayyip Erdogan has suppressed individual freedom, imposed strict censorship on the media, persecuted religious and ethnic minorities and attempted to destroy the strong secular traditions of Turkey's military, intellectual elites and bureaucracy, its *derin devlet* continues to be a powerful force. Ironically, in the case of Turkey, that may be a blessing.

If history is any guide, the *derin devlet* and its network of high-level allies in the intelligence agencies, military, security organizations, judicial system and organized criminal gangs are prepared to use any means possible to ensure that their own interests are advanced.

The Turkish "democracy" then, is only a front for a deeply entrenched network of power and authority.

Sound familiar?

Like the *derin devlet* in Turkey, the Deep State in America today tears down anyone who disagrees with its agenda.

As you can see from Turkey's volatile history, at the heart of any Deep State is secret collusion: An agreement between leaders, authorities, cultural influencers and criminals to use any means to maintain power and promote its agenda.

Ike's Warning about the Military-Industrial Complex

The concept of the Deep State in America was famously described in 1961. President Eisenhower warned Americans about the emerging danger of a "military-industrial complex."

The military-industrial complex is the close union of defense contractors with American armed forces. President Eisenhower warned that this entity threatened the survival of our democratic republic.

In a famous speech given at the close of his presidency, "Ike" explained this union of power as having potential for a "disastrous rise of misplaced power."[4]

He said,

"We must never let the weight of this combination endanger our liberties or democratic processes. **We should take nothing for granted.** Only an alert and knowledgeable citizenry can compel the proper meshing of the huge industrial and military machinery of defense with our peaceful methods and goals, so that security and liberty may prosper together."[5]

President Eisenhower warned the American people to guard against a force of power that could destroy their personal liberties and our Republic. And he told them to remain alert to the potential danger and lurking threat behind the military-industrial complex.

His admonition was to stay aware and preserve the constitutional system of government that serves the interests of the nation.

Although Ike's concept of the Deep State is different from what we are experiencing today, the danger remains the same. He knew that a bureaucratic system of power could ignore or oppose the needs and will of the American people.

President Eisenhower may never have anticipated how pervasive and dangerous the Deep State could become 50 years later. He may have never imagined that it would be driven by an ideology that is totally bent on destroying our social, economic and political structures and replacing it with a collectivist social, economic and political structure.

The Deep State in 21st-Century America

Today, the Deep State has become a pervasive and threatening reality in the United States. It has harnessed the power of the bureaucratic state. And it has used corruption and massive amounts of money to control technology, media and other powerful tools to impose its own agenda.

It's fooling many Americans into believing in an ideology that pretends to be pro-freedom and pro-equality. In reality, Deep State ideology is anti-liberty, anti-progress, anti-religious freedom and anti-American.

In the following chapters, you'll learn how prevalent the dangerous agenda of the Deep State really is — and how you can be aware, be alert and fight for positive change.

CHAPTER 2
Deep State Under the Radar Power: Government Employees

At its core, the Deep State seeks to expand its reach, maintain the status quo, stop change and resist anyone that disagrees.

Now, we must ask some critical questions:

Where does the Deep State get its power?

How — and by what means — is it effective?

How does it infiltrate the government?

Government employees are foundational to the Deep State's power, influence and authority.

The Deep State remains a stronghold because it is embedded in our government system. It's a sprawling network of individuals who abuse their power behind closed doors, with little or no accountability.

They cannot be fired, uprooted or told to leave.

Few, if any, really know what they are doing.

Government employees have the misplaced authority and funding to advance their own agenda … and resist anything that's not in their personal interest, or anyone who disagrees with their ideology.

As you'll see in the pages that follow, the nature of bureaucracy is to:

1. Protect itself.
2. Expand its size and function.
3. Avoid loss of funding.
4. Generate more tax revenue.

5. Avoid accountability and responsibility.
6. Now…To resist political, economic and cultural change.
7. Now…To promote opposition and undermine the Trump administration and his appointees.

In other words, the nature of the bureaucracy is to protect itself and grow itself. And now, the bureaucracy promotes a political agenda in order to create policies not authorized by Congress or the President.

Here's how the breakdown of the bureaucracy has created a system of manipulation and deceit to advance an ideological agenda in our federal government:

"Obama's Army"

There are more than 2 million federal government employees.[1] Out of these, 4,000 are top Presidential employees.[2]

These 4,000 top-level Presidential employees are followed directly in authority by an additional 8,000 employees called the Senior Executive Service — which acts as the critical "link" between key political leaders and the remaining 1.98 million government employees.[3]

The most disturbing part is that more than 7,000 members of the 8,000-member Senior Executive Service were appointed by President Obama.

That's why the Senior Executive Service has another name: "Obama's army."

This ideological army has the misplaced authority to control and manipulate incoming employees and managers appointed by President Trump.

Simply put, they can tell new political appointees

what they can and cannot do.

Driven by progressive ideology, the Senior Executive Service will distort the facts, hide vital information, and do whatever they can to effectively disregard the President's policies and agenda.

Most people don't know about this army of Obama-holdouts, entrenched in our federal government.

They also don't know that they are often underqualified and overpaid. In fact, each agency can set the salary of its members of the Senior Executive Service — with no top range.

The Senior Executive Service was dramatically enlarged by President Obama before he left office. These top level bureaucrats have become a dangerous tool of the Deep State — an arm of government employees with the power to disregard any change or progress initiated by President Trump.

Career Bureaucrats: Entrenched in Our Government to Advance an Ideological Agenda

The remaining 1.98 million government employees have made a career out of working for the federal government.

There is nothing wrong with making a career out of serving the government ... unless you abuse this role to protect your own power and self-interests.

Unfortunately, that is exactly what many career bureaucrats do. They want to maintain the status quo and keep their fat paychecks rolling in. They want to protect their power at any cost.

And many are ideologues, driven to advance their own agenda.

Career bureaucrats may be lazy, incompetent or

corrupt — but they can't be easily dismissed.

It's virtually impossible to fire them. They are safeguarded by government employee protections, "whistleblower" rules and union laws.

Take the case of the top-level employee at the Environmental Protection Agency, who was caught watching pornography for hours every day at work — for years. Investigators found more than 7,000 files of porn on his computer.[4] But because he has "job security," the EPA wasn't able to easily fire him. Eventually, he went on paid leave — collecting taxpayer money and probably still engaged in the same debauched behavior.

Hundreds of millions of taxpayer dollars are paying for policies that protect employees like this man.

It wasn't always this way in America. In fact, in the early 19th century, Congress required all federal workers to be reappointed every four years.

But Trump does not have the power to fire bureaucrats who do not share his ideology. Instead, they remain in their positions, trying to resist and undermine change they disagree with.

Obama appointees and holdovers include the thousands of people in their 20s who were hired by Obama to strategically advance a political agenda across Capitol Hill.

As you read in Chapter One, this army of ideologues was placed in power to create a total transformation of politics and culture. They are not driven by public opinion or by the will of the people. They are driven by a dangerous statist belief system that will not back down from its dogmatic positions.

Some of these ideologues include political

appointees that were "burrowed" into new jobs as career bureaucrats when Obama's term as President ended. That way, they were able to maintain power and continue to promote their agenda within the government — and not be ousted by President Trump.

One report found that 78 of Obama's political appointees stepped into career government jobs over a six-year period.[5] Many of these individuals came from the Department of Homeland Security, followed by the Department of Justice. Other departments that received an infiltration of political appointees included:

- The Department of Defense
- The Department of Agriculture
- The Department of Commerce
- The Department of Health and Human Services
- The Federal Deposit Insurance Corporation

All these government agencies are supposed to be nonpartisan and nonpoliticized. Yet, they were all permeated with radical political agents under Obama.

Many of these appointees have moved into career positions without receiving clearance or approval from the Office of Personnel Management. They are strategically placed throughout the government … fighting change, resisting progress and refusing to comply with President Trump's policies.

Obama appointees-turned-Obama holdovers are dangerous agents of the Deep State. They became career bureaucrats before Trump even moved into the White House.

Government workers like these "burrowed" officials are bent on manipulating policy to their own will. They directly or indirectly sabotage the President's orders and remain in taxpayer-funded power and authority.

Former Obama CIA Director John Brennan – who acknowledged lying under oath in testimony before the U.S. Senate – said, "I think it's the obligation of some executive branch officials to refuse to carry that out."[6]

In other words — resist.

As a side note, Brennan has a background in both Communism and Islamism, and he's proud of it.

Could his outrageous recommendation extend to an entire network of Deep State operatives that want to resist change?

Certain government employees within key agencies have picked up the slogan to "resist. " They resist any order that doesn't agree with their socialist, collectivist worldview or agenda.

Three Deep State Strategies

Here are three of the Deep State's strategies for resisting change in the Senior Executive Service and in the massive army of career bureaucrats working for federal agencies:

1. Strategic Sabotage

Deep State career bureaucrats — including Obama-era holdovers — will strategically sabotage any agenda with which they do not agree. This usually involves secretive communications to develop a strategic resistance, which maneuvers around the law.

Let's take a look at one agency where Deep State resistance runs at an extraordinary high level: The Environmental Protection Agency (EPA).

The EPA is responsible for issuing regulations, dispersing grants and funding scientific studies to protect the environment.

For example, during the Obama administration, the EPA issued highly restrictive regulations for power plants as part of the Clean Air Act. Unfortunately, this act raised energy bills for families, cut down on jobs and most likely has had little or no effect on so-called climate change.

The Trump administration has pushed for an EPA that seeks environmentally safe economic growth and reduces regulations that are unnecessarily excessive or restrictive.

But much of the workforce at the EPA believes that climate change is caused by human activity.

Trump's cuts in the massive agency funding and workforce have caused Deep State resistance. Employees have concealed information from the public and the government, and manipulated reports and projects to justify Obama-era policies.

They have even gathered to openly protest the new administration, encouraging others to "fight back" against the President's reforms. They have ridiculed office posters put up by the Trump administration — posters promoting the EPA's 2017 achievements. The president of the government employees union that represents many EPA workers even called these posters "propaganda."[7]

The evidence is clear — EPA employees form a bastion of Deep State influence.

Deep State resistance in the EPA is a dangerous threat to any proposed progress or change. It's also disturbing proof of how government employees are abusing their power.

Undercover communication "Signal" avoids government oversight

One of the most devious and secretive aspects of this resistance group inside the EPA is the use of a special cell phone application. The application is called "Signal," and it is used to communicate privately away from the eyes of Trump appointees in the government.

This strategic and secretive system of communication could potentially help a Deep State-infiltrated network of employees resist orders that don't fit with their own ideology.

"Signal" is especially effective at blocking the government from reading smartphone messages. By using this cell phone communication system, EPA employees make it difficult for others to monitor their work. "Signal" also impedes record-keeping and transparency.

Sidestepping Congress to advance an agenda

Deep State infiltration in the EPA hasn't only existed during the Trump administration. In 2015, Obama and the EPA basically sidestepped Congress to enact the Clean Power Plan, which Trump is in the process of repealing.

That was a powerful example of the Obama EPA maneuvering around the control of Congress to advance its own radical agenda.

The Clean Power Plan would have shut down hundreds of power plants and killed thousands of jobs. It would have also mandated a shift in U.S. power generation to problematic and incapable wind and solar farms. By launching it as an interpretation of the Clean Air Act, the EPA was able to overstep its own authority — and Congress.

The Clean Power Plan was backed by dubious scientific claims on how it would benefit the health of all Americans. The findings were scientifically flawed and politicized.

Likewise, their cost-benefit analyses were highly debatable. These were put into further question by the EPA's history of greatly underestimating the economic costs of its decisions and regulations.

Deep State government employees pushed the Clean Power Plan through to advance their own agenda. They sidestepped Congress and its constitutional authority to enact the laws under which the EPA operates.

2. Information leaks

Information leaks are a dangerous threat to America's national security. They are unconstitutional breaches of individual privacy …. and evidence of a politicized agenda within government agencies.

Any information coming from "anonymous sources" or introduced with "our sources say" often comes from Deep State government employees.

There were seven times as many leaks during the first 126 days of the Trump administration than during the 16 years of the previous two administrations.[8]

Deep State conspirators inside government agencies are responsible for committing felonies, including leaking classified information about the President's agenda, his conversations and his policies.

Even before President Trump took office, there were leaks, such as the Trump transition team's request for the names of Department of Energy staff who had worked on Obama's climate initiatives.

Details of Trump's plan to keep Guantanamo Bay open were also leaked to the Associated Press.

This is classified information, meant to undermine and embarrass Trump.

Deep State government employees have also used social media platforms like Twitter to undermine the President, which you'll read more about on the next page.

For example, the Department of Defense tweeted an article about a refugee from Iraq who became a U.S. Marine, just as the President was working out a plan to restrict refugees from illegally crossing American borders.

Just a coincidence?

Deep State-entrenched federal employees don't even need you to think it's a coincidence. Their brazen attacks are illegal. They are defiantly abusing their authority for their own political agenda.

By constantly leaking classified information, they hope to create a public perception of chaos in the White House. They want to erode support for Trump, regain control of Congress and remove Trump from office. They will politically destroy anyone who stands in their way.

And there is yet another way of resistance:

3. Propagandized resistance

Deep State-entrenched employees are motivated by their ideological beliefs more than anything else. Their ideology is more important to them than their duties and obligations, public opinion or their sworn loyalty to the Constitution and the authorities over them.

And in this age of social media and instantly

disseminated information and communication, it's easy to propagandize.

Deep State government employees have actually established rogue social media accounts. These accounts were created to "resist" and to embarrass the Trump administration.

These employees use social media applications such as Twitter to attack the Trump administration, using names like "AltEPA@ActualEPAFacts" to misuse information that is explicitly politicized, only a fraction of which concerns the environment.

Here's one tweet from AltEPA@ActualEPAFacts:

Hope Hicks (allegedly @realDonaldTrump's mistress) is a likely target for Mueller's investigation.[9]

This low insult came from deep inside the EPA.

Here is a retweet coming from the Department of Agriculture's rogue twitter account (AltUSDA@altusda):

So Team Nunes is admitting that Papadopoulos triggered the FBI's Russia investigation — not the Steele dossier?[10]

These tweets are blatantly distorted and politicized. They come from government employees at agencies that are legally required to be nonpartisan.

Rogue social media is not limited to Twitter. An unofficial NASA Facebook page (associated with the Twitter account @RogueNASA) was also set up to attack and discredit the current Administration. They publish posts and articles that rail against the President and spread fake news about him.

One post they shared was titled, "Donald Trump Didn't Want to Win — and Neither Did His Campaign."[11]

Of course, this has nothing to do with aerospace

— but it clearly shows that some employees at NASA have a radical, leftist agenda.

In the end, Deep State employees have an allegiance to a hard-left ideology. This is a dangerous totalitarian belief system that shuts down individual freedom and silences anyone who disagrees.

Far too many government employees have been exposed as a dangerous arm of the Deep State that must be called to account. They have:

- The insight to leak valuable information

- The power to delay or resist executive orders

- The influence to propagandize their own socialist, progressive agenda

These subversive agents of resistance exercise their powers to sabotage the President's agenda and manipulate policy for their own self-interests. In Chapter Four, you'll learn more about the system that enables this abuse of power: the massive, bloated bureaucracy.

CHAPTER 3
Government Agencies: Politicized and Transformed Into Deep State Strongholds of Influence and Power

In the previous chapter, we looked at the government employees who act as dangerous agents of the Deep State.

Entrenched in cushy, government-protected jobs, they use their authority and influence to promote their own agenda. And they abuse their power to tear down anyone who stands in their way.

In this chapter, you'll learn how the Deep State has infiltrated specific executive branch government agencies including:

- The Internal Revenue Service (IRS)
- The Environmental Protection Agency (EPA)
- The Federal Emergency Management Agency (FEMA)
- The U.S. Securities and Exchange Commission (SEC)
- The Department of Energy (DOE)
- The U.S. Department of Veterans Affairs (VA)
- The Equal Employment Opportunity Commission (EEOC)
- The Food and Drug Administration (FDA)

These executive branch agencies were created to serve the needs and welfare of the American people in a nonpartisan way. Unfortunately, they have been totally politicized by the Deep State. They are advancing a statist agenda through specific policies, court rulings and flat-out resistance to elected and appointed officials.

These agencies have been transformed — for the worse — by Obama-era holdovers in some of our nation's most powerful government agencies. And they continue to advance their own political and ideological agenda at the expense of freedom and integrity.

There are many more agencies that have the same Deep State problem.

For now, let's take a closer look at the agencies listed above — and their Deep State-influenced leaders and employees.

Deep State Targeting of Conservatives and Christians by the Internal Revenue Service (IRS)

The Internal Revenue Service (IRS) is responsible for tax collection and administering the Internal Revenue Code. They exercise great power when it comes to examining and taxing the finances of businesses and other organizations. They also bear the heavy responsibility of treating all businesses, organizations and individuals equally and fairly under the law.

Unfortunately, Deep State ideologues have abused this power to target organizations and individuals who don't agree with their big-government agenda.

Two recent officials involved in the IRS targeting of nonprogressive groups were Lois Lerner and John Koskinen.

Lerner was Director of the IRS Exempt Organizations Unit during the IRS's peak of Deep State-induced scandal. Koskinen was the Commissioner of the IRS and an equally deceptive bureaucrat, post-scandal.

Both were Deep State operatives whose despicable cover-ups revealed corruption at the IRS ... and they were just the tip of the iceberg.

The Deep State-Fueled IRS Scandal Under the Obama Administration

The IRS scandals during the Obama administration were so obvious and so outrageous that they were even exposed by the progressive-biased "mainstream" news media, including *The Washington Post* and *The New York Times*.

In 2013, the IRS released a report indicating that it did, in fact, deliberately target Conservative and Christian groups to delay their tax-exemption status. They illegally asked for unnecessary personal and religious information.

During the application process, the IRS had demanded donor and personal member information from these organizations — breaching their constitutional rights and further delaying the critical process of becoming tax-exempt.

The IRS even asked one pro-life group about the content of their prayers!

These illegal and outrageous actions took place under Lois Lerner's direction.

Ironically, Lerner is a past president of the Council on Governmental Ethics Laws.

In 2013, the IRS released a report indicating that it did, in fact, deliberately target Conservative and Christian groups to delay their tax-exemption status and illegally asked for unnecessary personal and religious information. Even Lerner admitted that what the IRS did was "absolutely inappropriate."[1]

The IRS abused their power in an attempt to destroy the First Amendment rights of specific organizations. And, their Deep State, Obama-appointed leadership lied in court and got away with it.

Former IRS Commissioner John Koskinen took office after Lois Lerner's appalling actions were exposed. However, Koskinen perpetuated the scandal by falsely stating in court that the selection of Conservative groups to delay their tax-exemption status was not in fact, "targeting."[2] Then, Koskinen told Congress that 30,000 emails from Lois Lerner had been lost.[3] This was a fact he intentionally withheld until it was absolutely necessary.

Later on, the emails were recovered by the Treasury Department Inspector General.

The shocking exposure of illegal targeting of Obama's political opponents, manipulation and lying left the IRS in disgrace. And, it provided irrefutable proof of politicized targeting by a government agency.

Targeting Franklin Graham, Christian, Evangelist and Founder of Samaritan's Purse

The IRS did not only prevent non-radical progressive groups from obtaining critical tax-exempt status — they also performed strategic audits aimed at discrediting these groups.

The IRS has worked to silence Christians, as shown by the 2012 incident involving The Rev. Franklin Graham, son of the late world-renowned evangelist Billy Graham.

In 2012, the IRS informed Franklin Graham that they would be auditing tax records for two of his organizations. Graham is an outspoken Christian evangelist and an ardent pro-life supporter. He is just the kind of highly respected leader the Deep State wants to rob of influence.

The IRS reviews came soon after one of Franklin Graham's organizations ran a newspaper ad supporting the overturn of same-sex marriage laws in North Carolina.

Do you think it was a coincidence?

I doubt it!

Deep State agents inside the IRS likely caught wind of Graham's opposition and use of free speech. Then, they targeted his organizations in a calculated and deliberate attack to destroy him financially — and keep him quiet.

The IRS will use their power against anyone who doesn't agree with their pro-abortion, same-sex marriage agenda.

The IRS is a bloated, inefficient agency in desperate need of transformation.

Manipulation and Deceit in the Environmental Protection Agency (EPA)

The Environmental Protection Agency (EPA) became a radical, ideological force under Obama, as you read about in Chapter Two.

Without congressional legislation, the agency destroyed business and property rights. They also ignored common-sense, pro-business solutions for protecting the environment. Instead, top managers in the EPA abused their power to advance a globalist, anti-free market agenda at the expense of the American people.

Under the direction of Obama-appointed Gina

McCarthy, the EPA instituted extreme policies to combat so-called "climate change."

McCarthy went so far in her zeal to advance the EPA's expansion of authority that she covered up the truth in court while testifying before Congress.

While explaining the details of the 2015 Clean Water Rule (which is an extreme overreach of federal rulemaking and a job-killing restriction) McCarthy lied about the availability of scientific reports backing the plan. She also downplayed the critical danger of hammering certain states with strict ozone rules and withholding of federal highway funding.

McCarthy lied in order to promote a Deep State ideology in one of the nation's most powerful and anti-business government agencies. She actively advanced a political agenda that opposes the free market and destroys the property rights of many Americans, especially farmers and ranchers.

President Trump has since begun the process of dismantling the Clean Water Rule, to the outrage of many Deep State operatives. They have tried to torpedo his initiatives, shut down progress and resist, above all else.

The Deep State is furious at Trump's efforts to downsize and stop the politicization of government agencies. This includes Trump's anti-bureaucracy appointments. They don't want anyone who will challenge the status quo or change policies that enable them to maintain their power.

The EPA is a battleground where Deep State operatives are advancing their own dangerous agenda in an attempt to preserve wasteful policies and projects at the expense of Americans.

Incompetence and Irrational Discrimination Against Christians in the Federal Emergency Management Agency (FEMA)

The Federal Emergency Management Agency (FEMA) is the government agency that responds to large-scale emergencies and disasters. These disasters include major hurricanes such as Katrina in 2005, Sandy in 2013 and Harvey in 2017.

FEMA is meant to act with compassion. But their Deep State policies have meant that the agency has often turned its back on people who really need help in an emergency.

Under President Obama, FEMA denied funding to churches and other Christian organizations preparing to help people rebuild after natural disasters. For example, "Project Paul" is a New Jersey-based nonprofit that provides relief and charity to the community. They were denied funding to repair their facilities after Hurricane Sandy in 2013.

Why?

Because the organization professes faith in Jesus Christ.

Hurricane Harvey in 2017 cost $125 billion in damage and was one of the costliest hurricanes in history.[4] But FEMA's response was often painfully slow … and cruelly biased against Christians.

Although FEMA had a budget of more than $7 billion for Disaster Relief for Hurricane Harvey, its inefficient and bloated bureaucracy left families without adequate assistance for weeks or months.[5] They had to make do with homes ravaged by disaster, picking their way through wreckage and dealing with dangerous conditions.

Churches were among the first organizations to provide immediate aid and shelter to victims of the horrendous storm.

While people waited for weeks to obtain basic assistance from FEMA, churches from all over the nation quickly sent volunteers to provide necessary aid and help clean up the devastation and destruction. Houses of worship, such as Hi-Way Tabernacle, even provided shelter and warmth for people in the aftermath of the disaster. Christians all over the world sent millions of dollars of free aid and provisions.

My wife, Shelly, went to Houston to help with Samaritan's Purse, a Christian relief organization. What did she see? Organization. Efficiency. Heartfelt compassion. It was a massive effort.

In the midst of this, FEMA turned its back on the churches who offered their help.

They would not rebuild church buildings, destroyed and wrecked by the deadly winds and heavy rains. Witch shops and strip clubs received federal aid, but churches? Not one penny out of $7.4 billion in FEMA funds was given to houses of worship.[6]

Why?

Because within those four walls, people praised and worshipped God.

FEMA's absurdly slow pace in responding to Hurricane Harvey ... their refusal to fund any efforts associated with religious organizations .... and their refusal to help repair any religious institution .... all exposed the Deep State's determination to advance their own agenda, even at the expense of the well-being of the American people.

This policy of maintaining blatant hostility to

religious groups has been denounced and stopped.

President Trump was shocked to see how FEMA was discriminating against churches. So, he ordered that FEMA change its policies immediately. Now, churches cannot be denied aid and funding for recovery solely on the basis of being a religious organization.

The Deep State bureaucracy resisted and refused to comply until Trump slammed down the hammer and got results.

Progress is being made ... but FEMA still needs to be transformed.

Destroying Business and Innovation in the U.S. Securities and Exchange Commission (SEC)

The U.S. Securities and Exchange Commission (SEC) is an independent agency of the United States federal government. Its role is to protect investors, maintain fair and orderly markets and facilitate the formation of valuable capital.

The SEC is basically the watchdog of Wall Street.

And because it's a bloated bureaucratic agency, it has often been a destructive force against businesses and investors.

It has become an army of agents who care about winning cases, not justice. For the SEC, collecting fines and fees is more important than truth and equity.

After 40 years of working with companies and dealing with the SEC, I've seen this agency destroy business again and again.

Even with the JOBS Act signed by President Obama, the SEC continues to manipulate the law and stop progress that Congress approved. Why? Because as an unaccountable agency, it can.

Obama appointed Mary J. White as the director of the SEC, with White becoming one of the agency's strictest and most arbitrary leaders with an ideological agenda.

White worked to enforce the disastrous Dodd-Frank Act, a massive 2,300-page law that exposes federal overreach at its worst.[7,8]

In the two months before White stepped down, the SEC collected more than $230 million in 23 corporate cases.[9] Fines – not fairness – were the objective. Business favorites and ideology were clearly the drivers.

White's priorities were to harshly and unfairly attack businesses at the expense of jobs and economic growth.

Not surprisingly, since President Trump took office there has been a dramatic reduction in penalties — from $702 million in 2016 to $127 million in 2017.[10]

But the SEC's Deep State army of lawyers and bureaucrats is still working to destroy pro-free market businesses and investors and advance their own interests.

Deep State Resistance in the U.S. Department of Energy (DOE)

The Department of Energy (DOE) is responsible for the nation's nuclear weapons programs, nuclear reactor systems for the U.S. Navy, energy policies, energy research, radioactive-waste disposal and domestic energy production.

Like most government departments, the DOE boasts

a massive budget ($32.5 billion in 2017) and a massive staff.[11] In many cases, both waste taxpayer dollars.

Trump has focused on reducing federal spending on renewable energy and efficiency. He is downsizing the DOE and bringing focus back to its original mission of nuclear energy research, development and nuclear waste clean-up.

But the Deep State is pushing back. They are specifically opposing the efforts of Trump to bring a pro-business and growth agenda to the DOE.

One of the Administration's first actions was to undo Obama's war on the coal and nuclear power industries. But it was slowed by the Federal Energy Regulatory Commission, a special agency within the DOE packed with Obama holdovers.

Deep State opposition within the department means that reforms – desperately needed in the DOE – may be delayed significantly.

Horrific Neglect and Incompetence in the U.S. Department of Veterans Affairs (VA)

The U.S. Department of Veterans Affairs (VA) is a cabinet-level department that provides healthcare and other services to U.S. veterans, including education assistance, home loans and life insurance.

The VA is one of the most bloated, wasteful arms of the government. In 2016, it had 372,614 government employees (approximately one-fifth of the total federal workforce) and in 2016, it spent more than $160 billion.[12,13] To give you an example: The VA includes a 3,498 person "police force" at their clinical and medical facilities. This "police force" cost the government more than $170 million in 2016.[14]

Even an overblown budget and huge staff haven't fixed this department's shocking dysfunction.

The VA has medical facilities and clinics that have been funded with billions of dollars by the Veterans Choice and Accountability Act. With this kind of financial backing, they should be providing our veterans with top-quality medical care and immediate attention.

But instead, those who have risked their lives to protect Americans have received shameful and outrageous mistreatment. They have been forced to endure months-long wait times for critical medical care — sometimes to the point of death.

In fact, one report showed that more than 307,000 veterans may have died waiting for Veterans Affairs healthcare.[15] In 2014, 37 veterans died waiting to be seen at a VA hospital in Louisiana while thousands more continued to wait to see a doctor.[16]

In 2015, more than 200 veterans died while waiting for medical care at a VA facility in Phoenix, Arizona, even after a 2014 investigation had showed that dozens of patients had died waiting for treatment at the same hospital.[17]

It's shocking, but under President Obama, the Deep State at the Department of Veterans Affairs actually tried to cover up the horrific neglect of U.S. veterans.

Employees at the VA were asked to black out wait times in official documents, so that their incompetence and deplorable performance could not be tracked — and so that the department couldn't be held accountable for its deadly inefficiency.

Inefficiency and neglect in the VA are still being exposed, as dozens of facilities and hospitals are being found guilty of often-fatal neglect and maltreatment of our country's heroes.

Individuals who have served courageously in Vietnam, Korea, Iraq, Afghanistan, and all over the world are being forgotten!

Take the case of Charlie Grijalva, a veteran who served valiantly in Afghanistan and Iraq. After serving, Charlie was diagnosed with PTSD and struggled with suicidal thoughts. When he didn't receive his medication on time from the VA hospitals, Charlie didn't make it. He killed himself in December 2014, just days before Christmas.

So, who's responsible for the mess?

Until recently, the Secretary of the Department of Veterans Affairs was David Shulkin, an Obama holdover who:

- Used his power to block veterans' access to private care hospitals…instead, forcing them to go to the overpopulated, inefficient and understaffed VA hospitals; and

- Performed a purge of employees he deemed "subversive"…in other words, those he didn't trust because of his own shadiness.[18]

Because of his resistance, Shulkin was fired from his post and replaced.

The Department of Veterans Affairs needs a major turnaround from life-threatening inefficiency and wastefulness. Their neglect of our veterans is disgraceful…an embarrassment to the nation and a clear indictment of bureaucratic incompetence in our government agencies.

A Radical Transgender Agenda in the Equal Employment Opportunity Commission (EEOC)

The Equal Employment Opportunity Commission (EEOC) was created to enforce federal employment antidiscrimination laws.

This agency has authority in both the public and private sectors — and plenty of opportunity to abuse its power. Historically, the Deep State within the EEOC has ignored the need for congressional authority and advanced its own progressive agenda through activism, using memoranda, legal "sleights of hand" and court actions.

Under the Obama administration, the Deep State took control of the EEOC to become yet another force of progressive ideology. The agency picked up the LGBT cause to spearhead an all-out attack on morality and traditional values, making the claim that sex discrimination includes "gender identity" and "sexual orientation."[19]

In truth, this is a manipulation of a law that was intended to protect the rights of both sexes in the workplace. But now, the EEOC has reinterpreted this law to include an extreme viewpoint that radically wars against mainstream America's traditional values and religious beliefs.

In fact, the EEOC website includes an entire page dedicated to the LGBT cause, specifically to transgenderism. They give a myriad of reasons a person can file for sex discrimination, and they boast of receiving more and more lawsuits every year.

One of the ways the EEOC is able to advance their agenda is through partnering with judicial activists. As you'll learn more about in Chapter Six, these are judges who will reinterpret the law according to their own progressive agenda.

Since becoming President, Donald Trump has appointed strict constructionists to the federal judiciary. These are judges who interpret the law in strict compliance with the words contained in the U.S. Constitution.

But still, Deep State influence remains rampant in this dangerous government agency.

For example, Obama appointee Chai Feldblum is still employed by the EEOC, advancing her anti-religious freedom agenda. Feldblum once stated,

"There can be a conflict between religious liberty and sexual liberty, but in almost all cases the sexual liberty should win. In fact … I'm having a hard time coming up with any case in which religious liberty should win."[20]

It's appalling. This is a basic denial of religious freedom and First Amendment rights, delivered by a radical extremist whose job is to protect "equal" rights.

It's a typical example of Deep State ideology: Self-interest, hypocrisy and extreme anti-religious bigotry masquerading as "compassion."

Government Crackdown on Life-Saving and Healing Alternative Therapies in the Food and Drug Administration (FDA)

Not only are Deep State ideologues opposed to pro-business legislation, they will even crush innovations that could bring relief to millions.

The Food and Drug Administration (FDA) is a government agency that uses its authority to place destructive restrictions on the sale of food and drugs. This prevents the growth of new business, job creation and life-saving and beneficial products available to the public.

One way that the FDA abuses its power is to deem alternative medicine products as dangerous and unfit for sale, such as Kratom. Kratom is a plant that is used around the world to relive pain, cure alcohol addiction and help alleviate mental illness like depression or PTSD. It has also been shown to be an excellent therapy for people coming off of life-threatening drugs.

However, the FDA has compared Kratom to opioids, claiming that it's killed 36 people. What they didn't mention is that these 36 individuals were also using potentially fatal substances at the time of their death.[21]

The FDA doesn't want Kratom on the market for one reason: Money.

Because it's a naturally grown herbal supplement, Kratom can't be patented and monopolized by pharmaceutical companies. There's no great incentive for the FDA to make money on Kratom...so they are trying to ban it.

It's disgusting to claim an alternative treatment that could help millions is as dangerous as a life-threatening opioid like heroin.

But that's what government agencies do. They disregard the general interests of the public in order to expand, manipulate and control.

Over the years, I have seen people flee to Mexico, Europe, South America and even China for new cures they can't get in the U.S. — because of bureaucrats interfering with consumer choice.

I've met and read about countless individuals who

have tried unconventional treatments the FDA would most likely ban. These treatments have stopped pain, cured illnesses said to be incurable and healed many.

But the FDA doesn't care. Their highest priorities are to expand their own control and fill their coffers.

See Chapter Seven for more information about how hypocritical, greedy FDA crackdowns hurt business and the American public.

The Deep State has infiltrated the top echelons of our federal government's most important departments and agencies.

Their actions, which include targeting Conservatives and Christians, committing felonies such as perjury in court, withholding lawful aid from churches, neglecting veteran care and harshly restricting business and innovation, are proof that the Deep State has dangerously taken hold of some of our nation's most important institutions.

Deep State operatives have seized the opportunity to manipulate the law, used massive taxpayer funding to advance their own self-interest and abused their authority to maintain an iron grip on power.

And American citizens are suffering the consequences, which include higher debt, inefficient services, harsh regulations and dangerous incompetence.

CHAPTER 4
The Bloated Bureaucracy: Fat Paychecks, Socialist Ideology, Waste and Inefficiency

As a business owner of more than 40 years, I have experience in participating in and managing a private bureaucracy.

I've also had to deal with government bureaucrats who have unlimited time, unlimited money and unlimited power to destroy any opposition.

I can assure you that a private bureaucracy will always outperform a government bureaucracy in:

- **Accountability** – Private bureaucracies must operate within budget and time limits.

- **Effectiveness** – Private bureaucracies are far more effective at accomplishing projects and tasks quickly.

- **Quality** – Private bureaucracies are able to fire employees who are not performing well, unlike government bureaucracies who are unable to do so.

- **Authority** – Private bureaucracies do not allow people to abuse their authority or power, unlike government bureaucracies.

In starting and running my own businesses, I've had to deal with the arrogance of government bureaucrats who think they are right and everyone else is wrong.

I've also seen the negative impact of bureaucracy on business. I've personally met government bureaucrats who are oblivious to the pain and suffering they inflict on real people in the private sector.

These individuals have no concern for constitutional liberty or individual freedom.

They claim to value transformation — but in reality, they only want progress on their own terms.

In this chapter, you'll discover why government employees who are unelected officials — "career bureaucrats" — are so tenacious in holding onto their positions.

They are the beneficiaries of the massive, wasteful and absurdly inefficient administrative state. It's what I call the "bloated bureaucracy," and it's killing enterprise and innovation in America.

The truth is, government employees have it pretty good right now.

So good, in fact, that their salaries usually put them in the top 10 percent of income-earners in America.[1] The four richest counties in the United States are suburbs of D.C.[2] ... because of the inflated incomes of wealthy government bureaucrats.

County	Median Household Income
Loudoun County, VA	$125,900
Falls Church City, VA	$122,092
Fairfax County, VA	$112,844
Howard County, MD	$110,224

To give you an idea of how the rest of the country compares, the national median income hovers around $59,000.[3]

The cushy jobs of government bureaucrats offer them job security and high salaries — regardless of how they perform in the workplace.

Many of these positions do nothing to contribute to

the American economy. Instead, they drain the nation's resources by enforcing anti-business regulations and expanding government overreach.

The bloated bureaucracy is built on an ideology that always fails: Government control of the economy, or socialism. Socialism only creates oppression and political and economic distortions. It discourages growth and innovation, and seeks to keep people under control.

But the bureaucracy doesn't care about results or outcome. It lives to grow and expand at the expense of wasting time and human capital — and your taxpayer dollars.

There are more than 18 million government employees today, working for a government that is three times larger than it was in 1960.[4]

The bureaucracy has achieved its goal of endless crawl and creep. It reaches into the lives (and pockets) of hard-working Americans like you. It lives to:

– **Defend** itself at all costs

– **Hide** its inefficiencies

– **Grow** itself continuously, expanding to "solve" problems that it has created with its own self-serving rules and regulations

In this chapter, you'll discover more about the ideology behind the "bloated bureaucracy." You'll also discover why this system is so dangerous to the nation (and you).

The Bloated Bureaucracy - Built on Socialism

The administrative state uses a massive class of professionals to oversee the government, economy and society. These are government bureaucrats with virtually unchecked power to make critical decisions and spend our tax dollars.

As you may remember from Chapter Two, these government employees can't easily be fired – if at all.

Many of the administrative state's values conflict directly with the core principles of American government: A constitutional democratic republic with limited and enumerated powers and reach.

The administrative state is anti-freedom and pro-government, and undermines the foundational values and Constitution of this country.

The bloated bureaucracy is built on these five socialist ideals:

1. A strong federal government. In the United States Constitution, and throughout American history, the federal government has been assigned a limited role focused on individual freedom, national defense, the administration of justice and religious liberty. But the bloated bureaucracy – and the Deep State – value a big government that continues to expand.

2. Overreach and regulations, at the expense of freedom and innovation. Socialism stifles innovation. It retards progress. For example, there's a new cancer drug that would never have come out if not for free enterprise and the profit motive. Investors and scientists expect to see as much as $10 billion in sales of this drug. It will make some people rich and save many lives. Innovations in technology, drugs and medical devices and systems require a free people who are not shackled by a bloated bureaucracy and unnecessary regulations. Can you imagine a bureaucrat — in the DMV, for example — inventing anything? They take, but they don't create. Socialism doesn't reward risk and productivity.

3. A top-down approach. Bureaucracies enforce top-down rules that hinder entrepreneurship and economic growth. Their rules and regulations ensure their own expansion of power at the expense of a healthy free-market economy.

4. A rich, ruling elite that drains the resources of others. Many bureaucrats have incredibly high salaries and cushy benefits, funded by your tax dollars. They earn a massive income by participating in a wasteful, inefficient enterprise. The bureaucracy accomplishes very little that is productive or necessary. Put the same amount of money in the hands of motivated entrepreneurs and the outcomes are completely different.

5. Centralized power. The genius of the United States Constitution is, among other things, that it is designed to prevent the creation of a centralized power that will result in coercion and dictatorship. The bureaucracy bypasses constitutional powers by creating a massive entity that puts power in the hands of an unelected, politicized elite.

Appalling, Massive Spending on Bloated Salaries and Bonuses

Here's what the government doesn't want you to know:

With each passing minute, the government spends $1 million on its federal employees.[5]

Every hour, the government spends $66 million on its federal employees.[6]

Every time you shut the lights off after a full day, the federal government has spent more than $500 million on paying its workforce.[7]

Funding for obscenely high federal salaries grew under the Obama administration.

Let's take a look at the numbers:

From 2010 to 2016, the number of federal government employees who make more than $200,000 grew by 165%.[8]

In 2016, one in five federal employees made six-figure incomes. Many of these incomes were for jobs that only contribute to waste and economic inefficiency.[9]

What's more, this kind of information is now being hidden from public view by being labeled or classified as confidential.

In fact, in FY2017, 254,839 federal salaries were removed from the Civil Service payroll, a 740% increase from the salaries redacted in FY2016.[10]

Most of the salaries considered classified are in the Department of Homeland Security, the Internal Revenue Service, the Department of Veterans Affairs and the Office of Personnel Management.

The Deep State doesn't want you to know how much federal government employees are being paid for cushy positions.

Let's take a look at a few specific examples of the government's financial wastefulness. These include paying absurdly high salaries and shocking bonuses that waste your tax dollars and drain the economy.

Presidio Trust is a national park and federal agency in San Francisco that pays 326 employees a total compensation of $28.8 million. This agency – basically a tourist attraction for visitors to the Golden

Gate Bridge – paid a bonus of $141,525 to its payroll manager in 2016, the largest such payout in the federal government that year.[11]

Covered California, California's appallingly wasteful arm of Obamacare, pays one of the top salaries in the federal government to its executive director. For running an agency that spends an obscene amount on marketing (which you'll learn more about later), has skyrocketing premiums and has failed to deliver on quality healthcare, Peter Lee is paid $436,800 annually. This doesn't include his bonuses which total tens of thousands of dollars.[12]

The state of California is collapsing under the weight of its enormous, growing debt, which exceeds $255 billion. This massive debt is the result of unfunded public pensions, retiree health care and bonds. Bureaucratic waste happens at the federal, state and local levels. For example, the average state/local federal employee in California earns more than $120,000 per year.[13] And, in 2017 California's state payroll grew by more than $1 billion.[14]

As you can see, working for the government is one of the most lucrative careers you can have. These jobs are funded by your tax dollars and rely on corruption and inefficiency to keep them running one step short of bankruptcy or worse.

Why Overregulation Destroys Businesses — and Your Personal Wealth

One of the primary roles of the bureaucracy is to regulate. They create miles of red tape and regulation that produce needless hurdles for everyone: Business people in the private sector, contractors and even government employees.

I was once asked on the Neil Cavuto TV show, "Craig, as a small business owner, what do you think the number-one problem facing businesses is today?"

My answer was not "taxes." It was not "capital." And it was not "interest rates."

I answered, "Neil, the number one problem is unnecessary and excessive regulation."

The number-one problem that all businesses face today is the government bureaucracy that is overregulating the economy, stifling innovation and killing jobs.

As a business owner that services business clients, I've seen firsthand how companies are hounded and destroyed by mindless, excessive and politically-driven regulations.

I've seen others prevented from potentially achieving incredible growth.

I've seen dreams destroyed, new jobs lost and greater incomes for employees never realized. I've seen breakthrough innovations and discoveries eradicated, all because of anti-business regulations.

Regulation stifles growth and entrepreneurship. It creates more work. It wastes time. And it wastes money.

There are 220,000 federal regulators, who spend a massive budget of $63 billion to impose rules. These rules make life miserable for many business people by burdening them with red tape, profit-killing restrictions and dangerous loopholes. Their role is to make the rules and regulations and enforce them.

In 1960, the federal government's book of regulations was about 22,000 pages. Today, it's 185,000 pages long, with nearly 300,000 rules that are set in place for you to possibly violate (usually unknowingly).[15]

Here's an idea of what's included in this "rule guide":

- Obamacare regulations alone create more than 10,000 pages of rules.[16] Picture a stack of eight Bibles. This stack would be shorter than the height of the book of disastrous Obamacare rules, which have been written and enforced at an astronomical expense.

- The federal tax code has more than 73,000 pages of regulations that stifle business growth and penalize people for committing innocent infractions and taking advantage of legal but debatable loopholes.[17]

While draining America of its creativity and potential, regulatory mandates produce huge amounts of money for the federal government. In fact, these regulations produce more than corporate, income, payroll, excise and estate taxes combined.

By conservative estimates, the total cost of regulation has been estimated at more than $2 trillion a year. That's more than $6,500 for every person in the United States.[18] This amount doesn't even include the "hidden costs" of lower wages, higher prices for goods and services, fewer products on the market and fewer job opportunities.

Overregulation makes it more difficult to innovate and create new products or services without jumping through government-made hoops and other obstacles.

Here's an example of what regulation does to a brilliant business idea that has the potential to create a valuable service, wealth and jobs:

"Flytenow" was an idea for a phone app that functions a lot like Uber, but for pilots rather than drivers. It connects licensed, private pilots with people who would like to share flight expenses in exchange for transportation.

It's a great idea, but the Federal Aviation Administration shot it down. They decided that these private pilots would have to be licensed like commercial airline pilots. This was a needless – and fatal – regulation on a business idea with great potential. So, Flytenow died in its early stages of innovation without ever having the chance to take off.

Today, there are nearly half a million Uber drivers who are able to make extra income and have made the start-up a multi-billion-dollar company.[19] Imagine that Uber drivers were required to become taxi drivers before driving others to their destinations. Uber never would have succeeded, and we would still be flagging down taxis at much higher costs.

As a central priority of the bloated bureaucracy, regulation is placing a heavy burden on businesses, individuals, the economy and the nation. It's stifling growth by costing us trillions and preventing us from creating wealth from new ideas.

Wildly Inefficient and Incompetent: How the Bloated Bureaucracy Compares to Private Companies

Government agencies have budgets and staffing numbers that most businesses can only dream of. But the government's performance shows that they are horribly run and accomplish very little.

I have personally encountered this type of destructive bureaucratic mentality many times. And

I have learned how wasteful, incompetent and anti-business the California State Board of Equalization is.

Many years ago, the Board of Equalization came to my business and told me I wasn't in compliance with a sales tax law (according to their interpretation).

Then, a bureaucrat showed up. He saw what he claimed was an infraction in which I combined two items that should have been on a separate piece of documentation. In short, I simply had not filled out an invoice the way the bureaucrat wanted.

For this, I received a $500,000 fine for back taxes. It was a fine that I could not collect from my clients since it went back for years. Not to mention the fine was completely unfair because I was in compliance ... except for the bureaucrat's contrary interpretation.

So, I went through the different appeals processes, and appeared before the final appeal board.

I told the presiding bureaucrat, "If I have to pay this fine, I may be forced to go out of business. I can't afford this type of outrageous and unfair fine, and there's nothing I did wrong. I was in compliance all the way through."

The bureaucrat looked me in the face and said coldly, "If you can't afford to pay your taxes, you don't belong in business. Case closed."

This terrible injustice set my business and me back many years. I wasn't able to hire new employees or expand. I had to pay off debt, because of one bureaucrat's power trip and anti-business attitude. It's this type of Deep State mentality that is prevalent within almost every bureaucracy.

Let's take a look at some examples of the U.S. government's shocking incompetence being paid for by your hard-earned tax dollars.

The United States Postal Service (USPS)

My ad agency has sent out more than a billion direct mail pieces for my clients. I have to deal with the post office as a constant, daily exercise.

And it's a nightmare!

Nearly every American has experienced the poor customer service the USPS delivers. And, by constantly increasing postage, they're actually killing off small-business entrepreneurs and even larger companies.

If the government regulations against private delivery were eliminated, the economic boom created by private postal delivery services would be mind-blowing.

To give you an idea of how the USPS measures up to private businesses, in the first quarter of 2018, FedEx made a net income of $596 million[20] ... And the USPS lost $540 million.[21]

The U.S. Postal Service is not a government agency, but it operates just like one: Failing, wasteful and inefficient.

The Postal Service is also the largest employer of federal workers, with a staff of over half a million people.[22]

It's a bloated and dysfunctional monopoly that continues to sink into debt with its shocking incompetence and strong resistance to change.

The USPS is reporting $2.7 billion in losses over the last year. This massive loss factors in $4.1 billion in unpaid employee retirement expenses...adding to a total of $121 billion in unfunded liabilities.[23]

In fact, the USPS has lost billions of dollars every year – for the past 11 years.[24]

In total, the USPS is facing a $65 billion taxpayer bailout.

The USPS is an outdated, archaic organization that sinks lower into debt every year because of poor business practices. For example:

- The USPS massively undercharges for package delivery. In fact, it would have to raise average rates by 40%, or $1.40, to accurately reflect the cost of delivery. And, package delivery is rising... up 16% in 2016.[25]

- When a recent proposal to use drones and driverless vehicles for package delivery surfaced, unions shot down the idea, even though it would have helped the USPS begin to reduce some of its massive debt. But, like any bureaucracy, the USPS does not prioritize innovation or efficiency.

- The Postal Service has prefunded 75 years-worth of retiree health benefits, the result of misguided and poorly planned legislation forced on it by Congress.[26]

The USPS also charges artificially low rates to Amazon, giving special favors to the most powerful megaretailer in the world. An independent study done by Citigroup showed that the USPS should charge $1.46 more for each Amazon package it delivers.[27]

What does Amazon do in return? They plan to launch their own delivery service, called "Shipping with Amazon." This will make it even more difficult for the USPS to make a profit, and for competitors to succeed.

President Trump spoke out openly against the Postal

Service's special treatment of Amazon, calling for the agency to raise its rates for the retail giant. He then issued an executive order to evaluate the Post Office's operations and finances.

What the United States Postal Service needs is an overhaul — and massive restructuring. It should function more like a business.

But instead, it relies on archaic, outdated practices to sustain employee salaries in a dying industry.

Covered California

Covered California is California's arm of Obamacare — a massive waste of taxpayer dollars that underserves its customers and reneges or under-delivers on its promises.

Covered California has a marketing budget that exceeds that at most Fortune 500 companies: $45 million for ads, $18 million for TV and $8 million for radio. It even spent $100,000 on painting murals which are totally irrelevant to providing healthcare.[28]

And these marketing efforts have resulted in reduced enrollment – adding up to a marketing cost of $73.35 per person. I've been in marketing for more than 40 years. This is an outrageous amount of spending on advertising.

Companies with similar budgets earn billions of dollars in revenue. For example, Oracle — a database-management company — spends $68 million on advertising and marketing, and it makes $37.4 billion in net annual profit. Or Nissan, with almost $100 billion in revenue, spends only a fraction of the advertising budget of Covered California, at about $26 million.[29]

Covered California is only contributing to a broken

economy and massive debt in the state of California.

Massive Budget with Little Pay-off

Many government agencies have budgets that most large corporations can only dream about. What does the government actually accomplish with its billions?

Here are a few embarrassing examples:

- The U.S. government spent an amount equal to Facebook's first six years of operating costs to create healthcare.gov, the poorly functioning Obamacare website.[30] Facebook is now one of the world's most powerful companies — and Obamacare is run on a system that has failed its "customers" again and again with shut-downs and glitches.

- The government spends 320 times as much money as private industry does to send a rocket into space.[31]

- Even the U.S. military spends billions and billions of dollars on projects that often never see fruition. Take the construction of the "Zumwalt Class Destroyer." There are three of them, and at $3 billion each, they are so expensive that they are rarely used in combat zones.[32]

Take a hard look at government-run programs in the United States: Public education, welfare and mail delivery. They are always outperformed by their private-sector competitors: Private schools and universities, private charity, FedEx and UPS.

The bloated government bureaucracy has mastered waste and inefficiency. It's built on an ideology that is doomed to failure – socialism. It pays its workers high salaries and massive bonuses with your hard-earned tax dollars. And it relies on overregulation and powerful unions to fund its own coffers and stunt business growth.

It is truly an embarrassment to the nation. Private businesses and corporations do far better at providing quality services. They also create jobs and revenue that don't add to a government debt that is spiraling out of control.

A bloated bureaucracy is foundational to the Deep State. The bureaucracy employs overpaid and underperforming government employees (as explained in Chapter Two).

It also protects a dangerous ideology, promoted by leaders in the top echelons of these government agencies (explained in Chapter Three). It's what helps maintain and grow the power of the Deep State – at the expense of your money, freedom and right to innovate.

CHAPTER 5

The Disturbing Weaponization of U.S. Intelligence Agencies: The Deep State in the FBI, CIA and More

There are more than 17 known intelligence agencies that are designed to protect the American people, stop terrorism and support our national security.

The most well-known of these agencies are the CIA (Central Intelligence Agency), the FBI (Federal Bureau of Investigation) and the NSA (National Security Agency). These agencies collect information to protect our security and freedom as American citizens. They respectively report to the Director of National Intelligence, the Attorney General and the Undersecretary of Defense for Intelligence.

But a mission that started out strong and patriotic has been corrupted by career bureaucrats and agency leadership. Intelligence agencies have been aggressive in driving ideological changes under Obama. They have also resisted Trump policies at every turn since his election.

In fact, the corruption and stunning revelation of how they tried to manipulate the 2016 presidential election are horrific and shocking.

The ideologically driven Deep State and career bureaucrats have infiltrated intelligence agencies on the top levels of leadership to promote:

- Dangerous security breaches that affect the privacy of Americans
- Illegal spying, violating the freedoms and

rights of individuals

- A corrupt attack on our Republic by trying to manipulate the agencies' immense power to destroy its political opposition

They have also worked to undermine:

- Freedom and constitutional protection
- Fair elections
- The legitimacy and authority of President Trump

With an estimated 5 million government employees and private contractors who have access to classified information, it's likely only a small minority are driven solely by ideology.[1] The rest are patriotic and try to be nonpartisan and carry out their duties without undue political bias.

Unfortunately, Deep State operatives at the highest levels of the U.S. intelligence agencies have turned respected and important agencies into hotbeds of radical partisan political power. They are bent on destroying the Trump administration and defeating anything that doesn't agree with their own radical agenda.

Tragically — and dangerously — this includes illegal, unconstitutional and unwarranted spying on innocent Americans.

"The Trump-Russia Collusion"... Engineered by the Deep State to Distort the Truth and Destroy a Political Opponent

The politicized investigation of President Trump's purported collusion with Russia has exposed the Deep State inside U.S. intelligence agencies.

That Deep State activity is now known as the

"Mueller Investigation." Led by former FBI Director Robert Mueller, it has roots in a corrupt collaboration among:

- Hillary Clinton
- The Democratic National Committee
- Former FBI Director James Comey
- Fusion-GPS founder Glenn Simpson
- Russian dossier author Christopher Steele
- FBI agent Peter Strzok
- FBI lawyer Lisa Page, Strzok's mistress
- Obama-era Attorney General Loretta Lynch
- Other high-level officials in the FBI, including Chief Legal Counsel James Baker and FBI Deputy Director Andrew McCabe
- The FBI and the secret Foreign Intelligence Surveillance Court, or FISA Court

Here are the four steps these collaborators took to spy on the current administration:

STEP #1: Wrote a politically fabricated dossier, using unreliable resources.

Deep State sympathizers were outraged that Trump was running for President. They feared he would dismantle their power structures and disrupt their ideological worldview, so they worked secretly to influence the 2016 election and then sabotage the 2017 presidential transition.

According to the FBI's Independent Inspector General, FBI agent Peter Strzok even said in a text message sent to his mistress and fellow Deep State sympathizer, "We'll stop [Trump from becoming president]."[2]

Deep State ideologues also created a fake document that would allow them to spy on Donald Trump. They used this document as false probable cause "evidence" that would be used in the FISA court (a corrupt abuse of power which you'll learn about later) to obtain a warrant to spy on Trump and his associates.

Christopher Steele is a former British spy who hated Donald Trump. He even admitted that he was "desperate" that Trump wouldn't be elected as President.[3]

And, Steele needed money.

Relying on disreputable Russian sources, Steele concocted a dossier comprising 17 memos that alleged corruption and misconduct about Trump and a conspiracy between the Trump campaign and the Russian government to interfere with the 2016 presidential campaign. The dossier was funded by Hillary Clinton and the Democratic National Committee. Clinton also paid Fusion GPS to hire Steele.

In the end, Steele made $168,000 from the fabricated dossier.[4]

In further proof of Deep State collusion, Department of Justice official Bruce Ohr, who brought the anti-Trump "research" to the FBI, is married to Nellie Ohr. Nellie Ohr was paid by Fusion GPS for an "unknown role" related to the dossier.

Former FBI director James Comey testified under oath that the document was "salacious and unverified."[5] But, he approved its use by the FBI to obtain a surveillance warrant from the FISA Court against Trump and others.

(Comey was also suspected and investigated for mishandling information, by using a private email account to "conduct FBI business.")[6]

STEP #2: Leaked the dossier to the media to create additional "evidence."

Steele then marketed the dossier to the media, generating a report on Yahoo about the alleged collusion between the Trump campaign and Russia. BuzzFeed also published the dossier, but did not reveal its sources.

Steele lied to the FBI (a felony) about whether he leaked the report to the media. He was later fired for this move and called a "less than reliable source for the FBI." [7]

STEP #3: Used the false dossier as "probable cause" to apply for and receive an unconstitutional surveillance warrant to spy on American citizens.

This politically driven conspiracy gained its real power from the FISA Act. This flawed and possibly unconstitutional act has opened the door for continual abuse of power and violates our privacy by allowing the government to spy on Americans.

The FISA Act has established and authorized the Foreign Intelligence Surveillance Court, or FISA Court. This secretive court oversees requests for surveillance warrants against alleged foreign spies or traitors inside the U.S. These requests are primarily brought to the FISA Court by the NSA and the FBI.

FISA is also responsible for "unmasking," the release of private information about U.S. citizens who have been accidentally caught up in routine surveillance of foreign nationals. This violates the privacy, freedom and constitutional rights of American citizens.

Between January 2016 and Obama's last day in office, there was a 320% increase in unmasking.[8]

In fact, under former Director of National Intelligence and admitted perjurer James Clapper, the intelligence communities unmasked 1,934 U.S. citizens in 2016.[9] Clapper is a dangerous progressive ideologue who changed the rules of unmasking in 2013. In 1992, only the CIA Director was able to unmask. Now, any intelligence agency under the executive branch can perform this abuse of power.

Hundreds of these unmasking requests were made by one person — Samantha Power, the former U.S. ambassador to the United Nations. Power is a Deep State ideologue, fueled by political motivation to take down her enemies and advance her political agenda.

Using this dangerous political tactic, Clapper, Power and others paved the way for the investigation into the alleged Trump-Russia collusion.

Under the Fourth Amendment, you and I are guaranteed rights to privacy. That means we cannot be spied on or searched without "probable cause." It means we have the right to keep our information private, including our phone calls and communications.

FISA, however, can allow certain politically motivated individuals – such as those in the intelligence agencies – to sidestep constitutional rights for their own gain and agenda. And that's exactly what the top FBI and DOJ officials did when they used the fake Steele dossier to obtain a warrant.

Because their investigation concerned foreign intelligence, Comey and his associates were able to obtain a surveillance warrant from the FISA Court.

They used the Steele dossier and the self-confirming Yahoo report to get the warrant without fully disclosing to the judges that they based their spying request on a fallacious Democrat political document and a media report leaked to news outlets by the author.

Comey, the FBI and other collaborators also hid what they were doing from congressional committees.

In July of 2016, the FISA Court refused to issue a surveillance warrant to spy on American citizen Carter Page. Page was a former volunteer and adviser to the Trump campaign. But on the basis of the Clinton-funded dossier and the Yahoo news report (fed to Yahoo by Steele), the Court issued a warrant in October of 2016.

To keep the court order alive, former FBI Director James Comey, fired FBI Deputy Director Andrew McCabe, fired Deputy Attorney General Sally Yates, Deputy Attorney General Rod Rosenstein and other top officials criminally signed three renewals of the FISA application. These renewals require specific findings of probable cause every 90 days to continue spying.[10]

STEP #4: Used a FISA surveillance warrant to spy on political opponents.

Some legal observers think the FISA court has become a dangerous entity with power as invasive and final as the U.S. Supreme Court. They also believe it has been abused to become a vehicle for illegal spying on American citizens. And in this case, it has been weaponized by supporters of one political party against another.

President Trump was ridiculed and mocked by

the media for claiming to have been wiretapped by the Obama administration. But he has since been vindicated, as reports have been released that prove his claims were true.

The U.S. Department of Justice (DOJ) stated that there was no evidence of Donald Trump being deliberately surveyed. But, they refused to say if the President was incidentally included in the FISA Paul Manafort wiretaps.

When Donald Trump began tweeting that he was being wiretapped, the liberal mainstream media went wild. They mocked and smeared him. But CNN has since admitted that Trump's claims were right: Paul Manafort, his campaign manager, and probably others were wiretapped in one of the most disturbing and outrageous political crimes ever committed by officials in the U.S. government against a political opponent.

Trump foreign policy adviser Carter Page was also wiretapped because of alleged collusion with Russia.

The wiretapping has also potentially caught up countless American citizens, including former Trump adviser and chief strategist Steve Bannon.

Now that you know some of the steps that were taken by the Obama FBI and intelligence agencies to ignore the U.S. Constitution and spy on President Trump and his campaign, let's look deeper into the sordid roots and details behind this Deep State-fueled investigation.

The Mueller Team: Partisan and Political

The Mueller Investigation is historic because of its corrupt, politicized attack on a presidential administration.

Never before have individuals within the intelligence agencies targeted a presidential candidate or president in a politically motivated conspiracy.

Never before have the leaders of agencies established to protect national security forsaken their sworn oath and engaged in treasonous acts against the U.S. Constitution, the American people and the rule of law.

Robert Mueller, the former director of the FBI and special counsel on the Russia "investigation," has been working to subvert the authority of the President. Mueller leads an inquiry into whether Trump or his campaign officials "colluded" with Russian efforts to help Trump defeat Clinton through a campaign of hacking.

We know that Russia wants to destabilize democracy in America — and throughout the world — but there's no evidence that they "colluded" with President Trump before, during or after the 2016 election. Russian TV (RTV) contains almost all liberal progressive commentary. After all, the policies of Barack Obama and Hillary Clinton allowed the Russian government to crush the rights of their people.

A group of Russians spent $100,000 to run "fake" news hurting every candidate running for office.[11] Combined, Hillary Clinton and Donald Trump spent $81 million on Facebook ads for the presidential election.[12] Spending a paltry $100,000 has no impact on Facebook — or on an election.

By contrast, Mueller has unlimited money and an army of lawyers. He can easily bring charges against President Trump by seeking an indictment from a Washington, D.C., grand jury, where 90% of the people voted for Hillary Clinton.[13]

Mueller has used the most aggressive Democrat

attorneys in the country in his investigation. Many of them are attorneys who worked previously for Hillary Clinton and Barack Obama. This is clearly a "hit squad" assembled to delegitimize Donald Trump as President.

Mueller's team comprises at least a dozen lawyers who are totally partisan, including donors to Hillary Clinton's campaign and other politicized players including:

- Andrew Weissman, a veteran federal prosecutor who said he was "so proud" and "in awe" of Deputy Attorney General Sally Yates for refusing to enforce President Trump's temporary travel ban executive order.[14]

- Aaron Zebley, formerly known as Mueller's "right hand" man. In 2015, Zebley represented Justin Cooper, Clinton's IT staffer who helped set up Hillary's home server and smash her Blackberry devices to render them useless if they were subpoenaed.

- Peter Strzok and Lisa Page, who exchanged approximately 50,000 texts during and after the 2016 presidential election. These text conversations revealed a disturbing opposition to then-candidate Donald Trump, and heavily criticized him, including calling him an "idiot."[15,16] Strzok and Page, who were having an affair, have both left the Mueller team.

Strzok and Page were also both heavily involved in Clinton's email scandal. Strzok was the one who changed the language describing her criminal behavior from "grossly negligent" to "extremely careless" — making it more difficult to prosecute her for the numerous felonies she committed.[17]

They were also involved in a hateful text message exchange about a pro-life march in Washington D.C. They even conspired to fabricate weather concerns in order to cancel the march.

Mueller's team includes Deep State officials and government employees who will stop at nothing to destroy Trump.

They are Hillary supporters and ultra-progressive partisans who use deception, manipulation and any means at their disposal to ensure that their own self-interest prevails.

New Light Shed on a Suspicious Interview with an Obama Holdover

The evidence for this disturbing operation has focused new light on an otherwise confusing and suspicious MSNBC interview with Evelyn Farkas, former Deputy Assistant Secretary of Defense in the Obama Administration.

During the interview with the liberal network, Farkas said she urged her colleagues to "get as much information as you can — get as much intelligence as you can — before President Obama leaves the administration."[18]

Farkas also said she was fearful that the new administration would find out how they had gotten information about Trump's alleged collusion with Russia. She continued, saying that she and her colleagues might no longer have the same access to that information when their "sources and methods" were taken away.[19]

Their "sources and methods" mean wiretapping and illegal spying – unconstitutional and corrupt methods and actions to undermine the authority of President Trump.

The Historic Nunes Memo: Corruption Exposed

In early February 2018, the "Nunes" memo was released in an historic exposure of corruption in the federal government. The criminally obtained FISA warrant that allowed spying on Donald Trump showed that the treasonous conspiracy included high-ranking officials in many departments.

Devin Nunes, the chairman of the U.S. House Permanent Select Committee on Intelligence, led the investigation of the Mueller team's illegal spying.

The Nunes memo specifically focuses on the surveillance of Carter Page as part of the Mueller investigation, showing that:

- Electronic surveillance of Page was not properly approved or vetted by the FISA court.

- The warrant that was issued relied on false testimony and a fake dossier that was paid for and disseminated by Hillary Clinton and the DNC.

- The application for the FISA surveillance warrant excluded key details about the credibility of the dossier and the parties that paid for it.

- The FBI and DOJ falsely claimed that they ignored partisan politics in the investigation.

Nunes also revealed that the FBI had violated its own rules in accepting the dossier as sufficient evidence for a surveillance warrant based on the Foreign Intelligence Surveillance Act.

The Democrats released their own "counter" memo, but it didn't refute any of Nunes' findings. The heavily redacted document failed to address serious claims, namely that the evidence against Carter Page had not been validated before being presented to the FISA Court.

Draining the Swamp – McCabe Fired, the Deep State Roars with Anger

The FISA scandal was just one more searing proof of years of Deep State corruption in the top leadership of the FBI.

One month after the Nunes memo was released in March 2018, Deputy Director of the FBI Andrew McCabe was finally fired after lying and getting caught.

McCabe was intentionally misleading when speaking about his authorization to release leaks during the Hillary Clinton scandal in 2016 — an investigation which he tried to shut down, clearing Clinton's path to presidency.

McCabe's misconduct was being investigated by the Justice Department Inspector General Michael Horowitz. Horowitz's investigation eventually led the DOJ's Office of Professional Responsibility to recommend McCabe's firing.

After all, McCabe was second-in-command to the director of the FBI. He should be held accountable for hiding the truth.

The Deep State was outraged, because McCabe was fired before attaining the special perks of his massive retirement — at age 50. They blame the ousting of McCabe on Trump, saying it's a politicized move designed to advance his own agenda.

In reality, Trump didn't even fire McCabe. The FBI's Office of Professional Responsibility made the recommendation to fire McCabe, and Attorney General Jeff Sessions carried it out.

But progressive ideologues don't care about the truth. They care about advancing their own political aims and protecting their power.

The same agencies that were created to protect our national security and gather critical information about foreign adversaries and terrorists have been turned into Deep State dens of treachery and treason.

U.S. intelligence agencies have been infiltrated with falsehood, politicized by a radical progressive agenda and weaponized against President Trump.

We should be spying on foreign enemies and terrorists, not on our own President and his administration for partisan reasons.

The FBI and DOJ officials who have corrupted their authority and acted criminally have betrayed their sworn oath of allegiance to the U.S. Constitution. They have brought disgrace on the intelligence agencies who employed them and violated our constitutional rights.

They also embody the false and seditious message that partisan politics are more important than our national security.

But that's the defining character and agenda of the Deep State. They aren't concerned about you, your interests or even your safety.

They are focused on their own self-interests and preserving power at any cost.

In fact, the Department of Justice and the FBI will even defy the constitutional authority of Congress in order to protect themselves.

After Congress made subpoena requests for critically important documents related to Hillary Clinton's email server, the firing of Andrew McCabe and the investigation into the Trump campaign, Deputy Attorney General Rod Rosenstein and others refused to comply with their request.

Instead, they claimed delays and redactions necessary to protect national security in their reluctance to expose the truth.

Mounting Evidence, Corruption Exposed and the Deep State Roaring in Anger

The Deep State is roaring in anger.

The evidence of corruption is mounting, and criminal misconduct is being exposed.

As Americans, you and I need to defend our rights and freedom as guaranteed in the U.S. Constitution. We must redefine FISA, to prevent this sort of shocking security breach from ever happening again. And we must demand integrity and transparency in our intelligence agencies.

.

CHAPTER 6

Warning: Judicial Activists are Legislating a Dangerous Far-Left Ideology From the Bench

As you've now read about in previous chapters, the Deep State impacts government agencies in an ongoing effort to stop change, advance dangerous progressive ideology and oppose anyone who disagrees.

It may surprise you to learn that the Deep State is thriving in another branch of the federal government: The judicial branch.

Judges are the most powerful arbiters of law in our society.

We rely on them to make decisions based on the U.S. Constitution and the fundamental principles upon which our nation was founded. The Constitution was written to define and establish our republican form of government. It was also created to protect and guarantee that individual freedom and rights are protected for every American citizen. It is the bedrock of America and one of the reasons our country is so great.

That's why the judicial branch carries a heavy responsibility both to the law and to Americans. They must interpret the law according to the U.S. Constitution and carry out justice accordingly.

But a dangerous trend has taken hold of the judicial branch. And when I say "dangerous," I mean something that truly threatens your rights as an American.

Judges at the state and federal levels – many of them appointed by President Obama – have used their authority to make decisions that are based on their own personal politics rather than the Constitution. They want to:

1. Maintain and enlarge the power of the State
2. Legislate their personal politics from the bench
3. Bypass Congress, voters and the executive branch
4. Resist change, especially coming from President Trump

It's scary, but true. Deep State judicial activists are legislating public policy and successfully advancing a radically hard-left agenda across the country. They are putting into place new "laws" and mandates that fundamentally deny your values and individual rights as an American citizen – like freedom, family, faith and free enterprise.

These judges are called "judicial activists," and they are some of the most dangerous, entrenched agents of the Deep State.

Judicial Activism v. Strict Constructionism

The responsibility of a judge is to interpret and apply the law based on the U.S. Constitution, state law and the common law tradition we inherited primarily from England and from our European forebears.

The role of the judge is not to advance or promote an ideology or political agenda.

Unfortunately, there are judges in both the Supreme Court and state courts who aim to manipulate the law and public policy to advance their own agendas.

Judicial activists are dangerous to our country because they legislate from the bench. And they've had a terrible impact on our constitutional rights, our society and our government.

Judicial activists are not concerned about your well-being or about the foundational principles that have made this nation great. They are more concerned about legislating their personal progressive worldview and radical ideology.

On the other hand, strict constructionists are judges who interpret the law as written. They apply the Constitution based on its original meaning. They do not impose their own opinion. Rather, they look at the text and help ensure its original meaning is upheld and honored.

Today in America, we have a dangerous number of judicial activists who believe they have the authority and power to rewrite our laws.

Numerous judicial activists have been appointed as federal judges by recent presidents — not just Obama, but former President George Bush and President Bill Clinton.

State judicial offices are also packed with those promoting and legislating an extreme liberal ideology from the bench. For example, former California Governor Arnold Schwarzenegger and California Governor Jerry Brown have filled the bench with such judges.

The result?

- Rulings that are deliberately unconstitutional (such as the ruling involving Elaine Huguenin, who declined to photograph a same-sex wedding and lost in a State Court — a direct denial of religious freedom. Learn more about Huguenin in Chapter 11).

- Legislatures that ignore the power of elected officials — such as President Trump's executive order cancelling Obama's unconstitutional policy concerning the deferred action for childhood arrival (DACA) immigration policy, travel ban and more.

- Attempts to advance personal value systems at the expense of safety and efficacy (such as Judge Nicholas' Garaufis' absurd legal imposition on the New York Fire Department concerning racial quotas — harming the NYFD and putting people at risk).

- The advancement of a progressive agenda and social engineering in America (such as the coerced acceptance of self-proclaimed transgender individuals in the military, promoting a transgender ideology).

In the following pages, you will also see:

- How Obama transformed the judicial branch with highly partisan political appointments and progressive ideologues

- Specific cases where judicial activism is shaping our nation

- How the Deep State has weaponized our courts to ensure that their political agenda succeeds

Judges are critical to a functioning Constitutional Republic. Their job is to uphold the U.S. Constitution and our laws. They are responsible for preventing government officials from violating the Constitution and trampling on our freedoms.

The problem is, the roles have reversed. Now, Deep State judges who have a statist ideological agenda are using their authority to drive social activism and economic socialism.

Let's take a step back for a minute and look at how the judicial branch works, and how judges are appointed.

The judicial branch functions on several levels:

- **Supreme Court justices** are nominated by the President and confirmed by the U.S. Senate. There are nine sitting Supreme Court justices today. Once a Supreme Court justice is appointed, he or she typically serves for life.

- **Federal Court judges** are also nominated by the President and confirmed by the Senate. Federal judges who exercise judicial power as specified by Congress in Article III of the U.S. Constitution are also appointed as long as they exercise "good behavior"...which, for most judges, means life (US Const. Article III, sec. 1).

- On the state level, we have both **State Supreme Court judges and Appellate Court judges.** These appointments or elections vary by state. In NY, the highest court is the court of appeal.

Obama appointed a new group of partisan federal judges to ensure his own political objectives succeeded.

Under the Obama administration, 280 judges were confirmed, which constitutes about one-third of the federal judiciary.[1] The majority are progressive ideologues like Obama, judicial activists who will violate or ignore the written law at their whim. When Obama came into office, 10 of the 13 circuit courts of appeal were controlled by Republican appointees.[2]

Now, more than a year into Trump's presidency, nine of the 13 circuits are controlled by Obama judges. And because these judges are appointed for life, their authority will last for decades.

Let's take a look at what can happen when judicial activists are in a position of power, and how they abuse that power to radically change public policy.

DACA: Judicial Activists Deny Constitutional Law, Legislate Their Own Opinion Instead

In the controversy over President Trump's efforts to end DACA, Deep State-allied judicial activists attempted to stop President Trump in favor of their own opinion.

In 2012, Obama ordered Deferred Action for Childhood Arrivals (DACA), which allowed some illegal aliens who entered the country as minors to receive a renewable two-year period of deferred action from deportation, and to be eligible for a work permit.

The problem is, DACA has no basis in federal law. In fact, it violates federal law. Federal law enacted by Congress requires that illegal immigrants should be deported from this country. Only Congress could modify the law. That being said, DACA was a presidential executive order ready for rescission by President Trump. Simply put, it was unconstitutional.

The Trump administration had planned to refuse new deferred action applications but allow current applications to remain in effect until they expire.

U.S. Attorney General Jeff Sessions announced the end of DACA on the grounds that it is an "unconstitutional exercise of authority under the executive branch."[3] Sessions said — correctly — that the Obama executive branch circumvented immigration laws and bypassed Congress to get what they wanted.

In a brilliant defense of the immigration law, which is continually distorted by judicial activists, Sessions said,

"Societies where the rule of law is treasured are societies that tend to flourish and succeed."[4]

Sessions is right. But the Deep State fought back.

In furious response, two Deep State operatives — the University of California and its president, former Secretary of Homeland Security Janet Napolitano — sued to keep DACA intact. Their case was brought before William Alsup, a U.S. District Judge for the Northern District of California.

Alsup is one of the most dangerous judicial activists in our nation. He flatly rejected the termination of DACA, saying that to do so was "arbitrary" and "capricious."[5]

Ultimately, this judicial activist ruled that DACA should continue because he believes it's in the public interest. In other words, he believes in the intent of his progressive worldview, not the Constitution.

A second judicial activist — Nicholas Garaufis, a senior U.S. District Judge for the Eastern District of New York — also upheld the ruling in a case brought by a group of New York immigration lawyers.

As further evidence of Deep State power, the U.S. Supreme Court declined to hear the Trump administration's appeal of the ruling to uphold DACA.

Judicial activists have taken it upon themselves to be the arbiters of beliefs, politics, economics and morality in our country. They believe that "laws" that were put into place by unconstitutional means can be protected and upheld.

Nicholas Garaufis and the NY Fire Department: Promoting His Agenda at the Expense of Safety and Efficiency

Nicholas Garaufis, the same New York federal judge who agreed with Alsup's preposterous defense of DACA, has made disastrous decisions on the basis of his personal preference, which is always to be "politically correct" and radically left regardless of the price.

Garaufis, who was nominated to be a federal judge by Bill Clinton, demanded that the New York City Fire Department fill a strict racial quota. He ordered the Department to reduce its focus on objective qualifications when hiring.

His decision came in response to a lawsuit that claimed that two of the exams discriminated against blacks and Hispanics because there were lower pass rates among racial minorities.

The Fire Department was punished, and under Garaufis' watch, they had to enact disastrous new rules. Instead of hiring applicants based on their fitness and ability to perform under pressure and protect lives, they had to hire based on race.

The result was an increase in the injury rate and a 10-24% increase in the dropout rate.[6]

Garaufis' order posed greater danger to millions of people in the City of New York and to its firefighters. It was so detrimental that it was reversed by a federal appeals court.

In fact, this judicial activist was so biased that parts of the case were reassigned to a different judge.

A Judicial Activist Blocks Trump's Ban on Transgender Individuals in the U.S. Military

In 2016, President Obama lifted the ban on transgender people serving in the military. Obama wasn't concerned about the enormous medical costs to the military that employing transgender people would incur (one study estimated the cost at $2.4 million to $8.4 million per year).[7]

Obama wasn't even concerned about the amount of additional red tape required by the policy. This red tape has complicated our military forces' duties, distracting them from their duty to serve and protect the nation.

Obama's goal was social engineering at the expense of military strength and power.

In 2017, President Trump made the decision to reverse Obama's disastrous transgender policy, and return the military to its pre-Obama strength.

He also ended the policy that required the military to pay for the surgery pertaining to gender transition.

In commenting about his decision, Trump said,

"Our military must be focused on decisive and overwhelming … victory and cannot be burdened with the tremendous medical costs and disruption that transgenders in the military would entail."[8]

President Trump's decision was met with outrage by the Deep State.

U.S. District Judge Colleen Kollar-Kotelly blocked Trump's ban, effectively undoing his decision to focus on the military's efficacy and strength. She abused her authority in order to ensure that her own ideological agenda was affirmed by the law.

A second judicial activist, U.S. District Judge Marvin Garbis, also blocked Trump's policy change. Garbis argued that the change was harmful to those already undergoing a sex-change operation. He also claimed that the government must be required to cover the costs of these operations with your taxes.

These judges are not concerned with the priorities of the military: Winning wars and protecting the United States.

No, the Deep State has different priorities. They want to socially engineer society with new legislation, overhaul laws they oppose and sabotage President Trump's authority as Commander-in-Chief.

How Trump is "Draining the Swamp" And How the Deep State is Fighting Back

When Justice Antonin Scalia died, President Trump was given the opportunity to appoint a new Associate Justice to the Supreme Court — a strict constructionist who would uphold the U.S. Constitution and the traditional values of those who voted for him.

Trump did not disappoint. He nominated Neil Gorsuch, a former Judge of the U.S. Court of Appeals for the Tenth Circuit.

With Gorsuch, the Court will take on a more balanced, strict constructionist profile and exhibiting judicial restraint.

Gorsuch is relatively young — meaning he can serve for another 30 to 40 years. He's well respected by both conservative and progressive jurists. And he has a solid judicial record on the following issues:

– Freedom of speech and the press

– Freedom of religion and conscience

– The Second Amendment

– State sovereignty

– Limitation of the Administrative State;

– Protections against radical environmentalism

– Common-sense immigration

– Economic freedom

Gorsuch's seat fills a crucial swing seat. If a judicial activist had been nominated, it could have meant disaster for the country, for you and for your children.

Trump's nomination of Justice Gorsuch was decisive for America's future and ensuring, among other vital principles, individual freedom and religious liberty.

President Trump has continued to keep his promise to appoint "strong and principled jurists." As of this writing, the U.S. Senate confirmed 42 judges nominated by Trump — 1 Associate Justice of the Supreme Court of the United States, 21 judges for the United States Courts of Appeals, and 20 judges for the United States Districts Courts.[9]

Trump is draining the judicial swamp — and protecting our freedoms in the process.

As a U.S. citizen, you also have the power to help drain the judicial swamp. Here are three steps you can take:

1. Vote in all U.S. elections. Vote for Senate candidates who will oppose judicial activism. The U.S. Senate confirms judicial nominations.

2. Vote for President. Exercise your right to choose the leader of our nation. Vote for candidates who will appoint strict constructionists.

3. Vote for judges. In many states, you can vote for men and women who are committed to upholding the U.S. Constitution. You can vote for strict constructionists who will protect your liberties as an American. You can and should vote for judges who will protect your rights.

The Deep State is fighting back. They do not want people like you – Americans who believe in the fundamental principles and limitations on government that are enshrined in the U.S. Constitution – to choose the judges who will make critical rulings.

In fact, former Nazi collaborator and socialist billionaire George Soros – one of the Deep State's biggest financial supporters – is attempting to transform the judicial branch into a tool for political and economic collectivism. He has funded a massive project to keep conservative judges off the courts and elect judicial activists.

Soros' Deep State-backed plan is dangerous. But, it shouldn't be shocking, considering the Deep State's never-ending desire to control, manipulate and expand their own power.

Stay Educated, Informed, and Empowered as a Voter

As a U.S. citizen, it's critical that you educate yourself as a voter. You can help "drain the swamp" of judicial activists who are socially engineering dangerous and destructive values with their politically motivated rulings.

In California, http://JudgeVoterGuide.com evaluates every judicial race in the state. If you're a California resident, take a look at the voter guide so that you can see which candidate should get your vote. You can transform your state, culture, and politics. Hopefully, the Judge Voter Guide can be expanded nationally.

CHAPTER 7

K Street and the Lobbyists: The Invisible Deep State Support Network

If you visit Washington, D.C., you may find yourself on a major thoroughfare known as "K Street."

K Street was once home to many of Washington's most powerful lobbyists.

Although many of them have moved to other locations, the name "K Street" remains symbolic of:

Unfettered greed …

Abuse of power …

…And a corrupt political system controlled by the narrow pursuits of large corporations, special-interest groups and power-hungry politicians.

Lobbyists are some of the most powerful people in Washington, D.C.

Many lobbyists use their influence for good. For example, they can identify unseen problems in legislation and support political candidates who will make positive reforms.

Unfortunately, many of them are also influential participants in the Deep State.

They are also some of the wealthiest people in the region surrounding Washington, D.C. — the most affluent area in the United States.

In order to exercise undue and dangerous influence, lobbyists:

– Manipulate policy for their self-interest

- Influence political campaigns to determine who is elected
- Abuse power to maintain control
- Push back against positive changes in government

In other words, Deep State bureaucrats and the agenda of lobbyists create a powerful alliance.

Lobbyists include lawyers, former high-ranking government officials and other influential insiders with close ties to special interest organizations, industry trade associations and other pressure groups that are the true power brokers in Washington, D.C.

They work for different industries, small and large corporations and the big union bosses who spend millions to persuade legislators to protect their interests in political processes.

Lobbyists support an agenda. These agendas are paid for by a group, industry or individuals who spend large amounts of money to advance or protect their special interests. It's true that they are exercising their First Amendment rights to petition the government. But, K Street has become a politicized entity that helps ensure their self-interests remain entrenched in U.S. policy and legislation.

The highest priorities of Deep State lobbyists include:

- **Special tax favors.** Lobbyists will fight tooth and nail to ensure that they keep benefiting from special tax cuts and loopholes in the law. They are unconcerned about how ethical these tax cuts or loopholes are, or whether they are even constitutional.

- **Special regulations.** Deep State lobbyists

prioritize unnecessary regulations or excessive requirements that stunt business growth. Or, they push regulations to protect themselves from competition.

K Street has become synonymous with corruption and greed. It is often seen as a stronghold of powerful political elites who don't care about the interests of the American people.

Where do Deep State lobbyists get their power?

How is it that they're able to manipulate and control our nation's decision-makers to get what they want?

In many cases, the answer is simple: money.

When I ran for Congress, I was unable to receive any funds from lobbyists to finance my political campaign. But my opponent received more than $2.5 million from lobbyists.

The lobbyists were pitted against me.

These K Street power brokers have massive resources, and many politicians' very survival depends on them.

Lobbyists and PACS — Funding and Manipulating Political Candidates

Politicians often help run their campaigns on money raised by lobbyists, PACS and special interest groups.

Most of the time, candidates depend on these funds for their political success. They end up pandering to those who funded them during their campaigns – and if nominated and elected – during their terms of office.

One of the ways lobbyists fund candidates is through PACS — Political Action Committees. PACS collect contributions from wealthy individuals and other donors, and pour them into campaign coffers.

PACS will often collect money from "bundlers" — individuals who organize groups of people to contribute money to an individual campaign. For this effort, the bundler achieves special status, power and influence. Bundlers can also donate money directly to a candidate or campaign.

The 2016 presidential election was one of the clearest proofs and indictments of political manipulation. This election pitted one Deep State-aligned candidate, funded and beholden to lobbyists, against one of the most independent candidates in U.S. history: an individual who could largely fund himself and remain free from the corrupt influence of special interest groups.

During the presidential race, Hillary Clinton raised an enormous amount of cash from lobbies. They funneled their money directly through PACS and special interest groups. And in response, she pandered directly to their priorities and their ideological interests, and not to those of average Americans.

Clinton's PACS and special interest groups included:

- Priorities USA Action, a Super PAC which raised more than $192 million[1]

- Future 45, a Super PAC that raised over $24 million[2]

- Correct the Record, a PAC that raised over $9 million[3]

- American Federation of Teachers, which raised over $4 million

- The Office and Professional Employees International Union, which raised over $500,000[4]

- Google, Microsoft, Facebook, Apple, and Amazon,

which collectively raised nearly half a million dollars for Hillary's campaign[5]

President Trump, on the other hand, was the first President in modern times not to rely on money from lobbyists — and to have no obligation or loyalty to them.

Trump did not want to be obligated to special-interest groups. He wanted to run a campaign that wouldn't budge on his promises or be swayed by political pressure from large donors.

In the end, Clinton raised $1.2 billion, including $217.5 million from Super PACs. Trump raised $646.8 million, including $82.3 million from Super PACs. Clinton out-fundraised Trump by more than $544 million – and still lost.[6]

The presidential race was an embarrassment to the lobbyists and special interest groups that smugly believed they could maintain their power with cash.

But fundraising isn't limited to presidential candidates.

Members of the House and Senate also raise millions from PACS to keep their seats – and also pander to the lobbyists who help them stay in power.

In the following pages, you'll learn more shocking examples of how lobbyists have wielded dangerous control over our government. You'll learn how they have hindered innovation, damaged the free-market economy and defied President Trump's administration.

Deep State Lobbyists helped secure the auto-industry bailout, while saving their own union benefits.

Here's a powerful example of how special-interest groups – like big unions – will fund political campaigns to ensure their own security:

Obama was given around $400 million from big labor unions during the 2008 election — unions such as the United Automobile Workers (UAW).[7] So, when the auto industry had to be bailed out because of its failure in business and manufacturing — largely because of union power and weak management — Obama responded by finishing what Bush had started: A $17.4 billion bailout, in addition to $25 billion loaned to the industry by Congress months earlier.[8,9]

That bailout included terms that saved the pensions of UAW workers, but not those of nonunion workers. The politically driven terms resulted in the closure of non-UAW shops, while UAW factories were rescued.

Obama's move – which was seen by some as heroic — was really a political play. And nonunion workers in the automobile industry saw right through it.

With pro-union backing like this from powerful elected officials, it's no wonder that special interest groups pour money into the political campaigns of candidates who will pander to them.

Deep State Lobbyists watered down Trump's Tax Cut and Jobs Act.

The Deep State wanted everyone to believe that Trump's tax reform plan was going to benefit the wealthy at the expense of the middle class. They wanted people to believe Trump designed it to boost his own businesses.

In reality, Trump's taxcut was designed to boost the economy and the incomes of all Americans. It was created to generate jobs and to reduce the heavy burden of taxes on businesses and individuals.

The Tax Cuts and Jobs Act (TCJA) is boosting the after-tax incomes of taxpayers in every tax bracket.

Some very wealthy individual taxpayers and a number of taxpayers living in high-tax states may owe more taxes for 2017. In fact, President Trump has said that he's one of them.

But, at least 80 percent of American taxpayers are receiving a tax cut.[10]

But a significant number of Deep State lobbyists from big businesses and special interest groups railed against the Trump tax cuts.

Why?

The legislation closed the loopholes that had kept money in their pockets.

Large business groups, including the pharmaceutical industry and others, knew that they wouldn't get the tax breaks they once received under Trumps' new tax cut plan. So, they fought tooth and nail – spending millions of dollars – to preserve their interests in the final plan.

Senate and House leaders were overwhelmed by complaints from many Deep State constituencies. Special interest groups hounded them endlessly.

Congressman Mike Simpson from Idaho said,

"Some of my best supporters, associations and stuff, don't like provisions in this tax cut … Every association that I know of has come into my office and said 'you know this tax reform is really important, we got to get this done except this one provision here.'"[11]

The lobbyists failed to stop Trump's tax cut plan completely, but they fought for changes to protect their own interests. In the final version of the legislation, they helped preserve some provisions that were less damaging to their clients – ultimately undercutting the tax cut plan.

Deep State Lobbyists successfully fought the repeal of Obamacare.

Obamacare has been a healthcare monstrosity doomed to failure from the start. Its harmful and costly mandates, arbitrary regulations and government-controlled prices cause Americans to suffer because of:

- Inferior healthcare coverage
- Skyrocketing premiums
- Outrageous deductibles
- Lack of choices and competition in healthcare services and costs

Obamacare has cost Americans $1 trillion in tax increases , over $2 billion wasted on the Obamacare website disaster and the loss of millions of jobs. It has also advanced socialism and expanded the regulatory bureaucracy.[12,13]

Obamacare has been a massive failure and a horrible disaster for the American people.

However, Trump's plan to repeal Obamacare failed because of the lobbyists who worked to keep Obamacare in place, with massive amounts of money from special interest groups.

Doctors and hospitals knew that changes and cuts in insurance subsidies would affect their bottom lines, so they fought Trump's plan to dismantle Obamacare.

When Congress passed the so-called Affordable Care Act in 2010, they gave special favors to every part of the healthcare industry to get the legislation passed.

Eventually, many politicians succumbed to the pressure from lobbyists, and, in the end, this horrific legislation was kept in place.

Deep State lobbyists have fought to prevent the growth of business, innovation and entrepreneurship.

Lobbying groups from specific industries use their power to lobby government agencies to pass legislation that makes new business growth next to impossible.

Let's take a look at one example from the healthcare industry.

More than half of all Americans suffer from some kind of chronic illness.[14] And, one in six U.S. adults experience some kind of mental illness.[15] We should be encouraging innovation in healthcare, not using the same, expensive drugs that are making people poorer and even sicker with horrific side effects.

But the pharmaceutical companies have a lot of power...and lots of money.

The U.S. pharmaceutical market accounts for more than 45% of the world market, an amount worth more than $445 billion.[16]

Along with biotechnology and medical-device

companies, the pharmaceutical industry exercises enormous influence over the Food and Drug Administration (FDA). The FDA determines what drugs and devices may be legally sold in the United States.

For example, when it became clear that CBD — the non-mind-altering compound in cannabis — has incredible healing properties for chronic conditions, the pharmaceutical industry stepped in to create a monopoly on the compound.

In South Dakota, the pharmaceutical company GW Pharmaceuticals lobbied for a provision in a new law that legalized CBD. This new law had the potential to change the lives of tens of thousands of state residents, but the lobbyists' provision required new CBD products to be FDA-approved — a strict regulation that could only be met by GW'S own product.

Lobbyists from Big Pharma support government agencies with the power to pass arbitrary regulations. This keeps out competition. And only large corporations can afford to manage these unfair regulations.

Only the lobbyists, the pharmaceutical companies and the government agencies "win" in this scenario. Business and innovation are hindered, and Americans are left with fewer options and reduced access to the healthcare they desperately need.

Deep State Lobbyists include radical unions that want to promote socialism.

Some of the most powerful lobbyists include Big Union bosses. Some of these bosses spend tens of millions every year on advertising campaigns and political persuasion.

Collectively, the unions outspend individual donors, special interest groups and other lobbyists during election cycles. In fact, in 2012 the labor unions spent $1.7 billion on lobbying, dwarfing the famous Koch Brothers' $490 million.[17]

They also spend billions on their own political activity and on persuading union members to vote a specific way.

Sadly, unions too often promote progressive agendas and socialism that most of their members oppose. The aim of the leadership is often to promote a political agenda, not just work for wage increases and other issues employees support.

To ensure that they achieve their socialist ideals, they pay professional lobbyists or have their own lobbyists persuade our nation's most powerful politicians to support their agendas.

The largest trade union of public employees in the United States is the American Federation of State, County and Municipal Employees (AFSCME). The AFSCME represents 1.6 million employees and retirees in the public sector.[18] In fact, the majority of union members now work for the government.

The AFSCME consistently lobbies for socialist policies, including:

- **Single-payer healthcare,** a healthcare system totally controlled by the government. This system has reduced healthcare quality and options, longer wait times and ultimately results in more sickness. We've already seen the beginning of this nightmare with Obamacare.

- **Inflated pension benefits** that are sinking the nation into deeper and deeper debt.

- **Raising the minimum wage,** a harmful government regulation that is decreasing employment opportunities for minority youth, killing jobs and innovation and accelerating automation.

- **Fighting the privatization of government jobs,** which would, in practice, improve efficiency and cost. Like the bloated bureaucracy, the Big Union bosses want to protect their cushy jobs and benefits at the expense of the other workers, consumers and economy.

George Meany, former president of the American Federation of Labor and Congress of Industrial Organizations, said of government unions, "It is impossible to bargain collectively with the government."[19]

Even President Franklin D. Roosevelt said it was "unthinkable and intolerable" that government unions should go on strike.[20]

Even on the state level, unions influence the government by controlling the politicians. For example, the California unions are so powerful that no state-level politician can successfully oppose their agenda.

Unions are some of the most dangerous, politicized entities in the nation. They use lobbying to advance their anti-business, socialist agenda in the top echelons of America's decision-making bodies.

Deep State Lobbyists and Donald Trump

Lobbyists have the power to manipulate some political campaigns. They are able to help determine who will be put into office — and what they will support when they get there.

When politicians pander to Deep State lobbyists to get money, the democratic process is destroyed. Policy-making is no longer in the hands of those who are elected by the citizens. Instead, it's in the hands of a political elite with a powerful and dangerous agenda.

But there has been at least one exception to the corruption and pandering that have made a mockery of our political system. President Donald Trump could not be controlled by the lobbyists, even with all their money.

As you learned on previous pages, Trump largely funded his own campaign because of his incredible success in business. He was able to run unhindered by outside influence.

Voters knew that Trump didn't pander to special interest groups, and that he wouldn't flip-flop because of what his donors wanted.

They knew he would stand firm on his own program for policy change.

Trump won on his own by gaining the firm support of the American people and by funding his own campaign.

He has enacted a lobbying ban that prevents government officials from lobbying the agency where they worked for five years after they leave.[21]

Trump's step is a decisive move to "drain the swamp." But he continues to contend with a powerful coalition of Deep State lobbyists that have fought nearly every reform he has made.

It's a small but significant step. And more needs to be done.

CHAPTER 8

Establishment Republicans: Uneasy Deep State Allies Betraying Basic Principles

The Deep State is typically promoted by those with a progressive agenda.

But I want you to know this: The Deep State is not partisan. It's ideological.

If you identify as politically conservative or Libertarian, you need to know that just because some politicians call themselves Republicans, it doesn't mean that they share your values. It doesn't even mean they share your opinions on the best policies for our nation.

There are men and women who profess to be Republicans, but who are complicit in a dangerous framework of values that is pitted against freedom, family and the United States Constitution.

"Establishment Republicans" are the political Conservatives who are Republican in name only. They are often called RINOs (Republicans in Name Only). Like the government employees who are primarily interested in maintaining the status quo, Establishment Republicans use their authority and influence for their own benefit.

Their primary objective is not to support their constituents or the principles they run on. Their goal is to win the next election or satisfy a special interest group.

Establishment Republicans pretend to support

deregulation, downsizing the government and cutting the deficit.

But what they really are promoting is a permanent political elite that will remain in control. And they do so by:

- Supporting government expansion and objecting to downsizing
- Supporting new regulation and objecting to allowing the free market to operate
- Supporting taxes and not allowing people to keep what they earn

Establishment Republicans oppose the true Conservative and Libertarian principles of limited, small government, individual freedom and economic liberty and opportunity. In reality, they are more sympathetic to the bloated bureaucracy, which you read about in Chapter Four. They want to keep their positions of power and cushy benefits at any cost.

Here is how the unholy alliance of the Deep State and Establishment Republicans operates. There are five little-known strategies you should remember:

STRATEGY #1: Catering to the Establishment

Establishment Republicans have earned their nickname by catering to a system of entrenched political power rather than to the American people.

They will abandon values and principles of economic freedom and free market enterprise in a moment to win favor with the "establishment." In fact, they see doing so as a positive thing.

Arizona Senator and former presidential nominee John McCain is one of the most outspoken Establishment

Republicans. McCain openly admits that he hopes "establishment" politicians will influence President Trump in his decision-making.

During the 2008 presidential election, McCain flip-flopped on dozens of issues. These included his stance on abortion, privatizing Social Security, wiretapping, lobbying reform, the estate tax and the war in Iraq. The list goes on and on.

McCain's pandering shows his true nature as the quintessential Establishment Republican. He changes his mind according to what he thinks will benefit the existing establishment.

STRATEGY #2: Refusing to endorse Trump during the 2016 presidential election

Many Establishment Republicans were horrified that Trump was nominated for President.

They knew Trump was one politician they could not manipulate. They also knew that Trump would not back away from his policies and promises, even under pressure from the Deep State within his own party.

They also knew that Trump would shake up the political system. He wouldn't play "the game" that helps Establishment Republicans and other members of the Deep State maintain their plum benefits and corrupt power.

The following Establishment Republicans are just a few who attacked Trump in an effort to undermine his campaign for the presidency:

> – **Colin Powell (R)**, former Secretary of State under George W. Bush and an unabashed RINO, openly criticized President Trump for his policy on illegal immigration. Powell

announced he would vote for Hillary. Powell is the epitome of a Republican in Name Only. He has endorsed Obama twice, and was in favor of the Iran nuclear deal. Powell mocked Trump, saying, "he has insulted America in one way or another almost every day."[1]

- **Mitt Romney (R)**, former governor of Massachusetts and Republican nominee for President in 2012, verbally attacked Trump as his party's 2016 nominee. Romney called Trump a "phony" and "fraud."[2]

- **Michael Bloomberg (R)**, former Democrat who was elected mayor of New York as a Republican, opposes Trump so much that he gave an address at the Democratic National Committee in support of Clinton, saying that she should defeat Trump.

- **Chris Shays (R)**, former member of the House of Representatives, wrote an op-ed for CNN titled, "Why I'm Voting for Hillary Clinton." In it, Shays said Trump "represents practically everything I was taught not to be." [3]

Establishment Republicans who did not endorse Trump were threatened by the possibility of change. So, they smeared him in a desperate attempt to maintain the status quo. Their strategy of attacking Trump failed, and they were horrified when he was elected.

STRATEGY #3: Causing division in the Republican Party

When Establishment Republicans failed to prevent Trump from being elected as President, they moved to a second strategy: Stir up division within the GOP.

Arizona Senator Jeff Flake has been one of the biggest pot-stirrers. Flake divisively announced on the Senate floor that he wouldn't be seeking re-election.

Flake knew he wouldn't be re-elected anyway. So, in a last-ditch attempt to advance his agenda, he delivered a hate-filled speech in which he tried to convince others that Trump is somehow endangering the nation by taking on the liberal media.

During the speech, he compared Trump's language to that of Stalin. He accused him of inspiring dictators and attacked Trump for criticizing the press – even though the majority of media is openly biased in their treatment of Trump.

Flake's attacks on the President were met with mixed responses from the Republican Party. Many Republicans were outraged by the speech. Chairwoman of the Republican National Committee, Ronna Romney McDaniel, said of his diatribe that he had "gone too far."[4]

On the other hand, Flake's angry rhetoric caused further internal discord in the Republican Party. He has been joined by other Establishment Republicans in attacking Trump's character, such as Tennessee Senator Bob Corker.

Establishment Republicans deliberately sow discord and discontent, especially to advance their own agendas.

STRATEGY #4: Resisting policy change

Like government bureaucrats, Establishment Republicans oppose change.

Change might mean they will lose votes and their lavish lifestyles.

Change might mean that someone will expose the political hypocrisy and corruption that keeps them in power.

Establishment Republicans don't want individual defenders of freedom and free enterprise in power that would downsize and hold accountable the bureaucracy. They want an alternative to the Democratic Party push towards socialism...but maintain the status quo.

That's why it was a Republican – Arizona Senator John McCain – who ultimately killed the Obamacare repeal in 2017.

In his ultimate flip-flop, John McCain cost his party a victory that would have repealed Obamacare and laid the groundwork for creating a free market healthcare system — eliminating the bloated bureaucracy.

Originally, McCain supported a bill that would reform Obamacare. In fact, he ran on a political platform that promised to repeal and replace Obamacare.

But when healthcare reform bills were introduced in the Senate, McCain voted against them. In the last attempt by the GOP to replace Obamacare in the Graham-Cassidy Bill, McCain was the final "no" vote, delivering the fatal blow to repealing and replacing the law.

Animated by personal hatred for Trump and never reliable in his commitment to the Republican Party's values, McCain proved once again that he is a RINO and helped maintain a healthcare system that has been disastrous for the entire nation.

STRATEGY #5: Betraying Republican values

The Republican Party has supported conservative and Libertarian values of protecting constitutional rights, the free market, and reducing taxes, regulations and government control.

Republicans also traditionally support a limited government and slashing government waste and bureaucracy.

But the conservative and libertarian values and principles that most Republicans adhere to are opposed by Establishment Republicans.

This is seen on the state level as well.

For example, former Republican leader of the California State Senate Chad Mayes is yet another blatant example of an Establishment Republican. Mayes has betrayed the party's values of freedom, individual support for the U.S. Constitution and religious liberty.

While Trump rolled back disastrous environmental regulations that suppress economic freedom, Mayes aligned himself with progressive, Democrat leaders who wanted to extend Governor Jerry Brown's disastrous cap-and-trade scheme. This policy forces companies to buy permits to release greenhouse gases, destroys jobs and businesses and increases restrictive government regulations and power.

Mayes' support for Governor Brown's radical environmental policies raises gasoline prices by up to $0.79 a gallon by 2030.[5]

Mayes even delivered the deciding vote that extended the cap-and-trade program, betraying those who worked so hard for lower taxes and limited government. As a result, Mayes was asked by the

California Republican Party's board to step down as leader of the California State Assembly.

But Mayes hasn't stopped his active opposition to pro-business, pro-freedom and pro-family values. Along with former California Governor Arnold Schwarzenegger and Ohio Governor John Kasich, Mayes has pioneered a new program for the Republican Party in California called "New Way." This disastrous set of policies betrays values of freedom, panders to the progressive movement and strengthens the Deep State.

Schwarzenegger has disappointed his party again and again. As Governor of California, he pushed through cap-and-trade and helped pass the first across-the-board increase in sales and income taxes in 17 years. Schwarzenegger supported amnesty for illegal aliens. This has significantly increased an influx of illegal immigrants that has cut down on jobs for citizens and has made a reasonable standard of living nearly impossible for California's middle class.

Incidentally, Schwarzenegger also increased taxes, regulations and anti-family policies. Finally, he appointed judicial activists to the bench. In fact, over 80% of all his judicial nominees legislate the Deep State agenda from the bench.

Establishment Republicans will often compromise their core values for the sake of:
- Hefty campaign contributions
- Gaining favor with the lobbying industries
- Pandering to special interests to win popularity

Establishment Republicans won't uphold and promote your values and principles because they don't really care about them.

Ultimately, they want to resist progress, maintain power and status and use the political system for personal gain.

CHAPTER 9

Unseen, Unknown, Unaccountable! The Unholy Alliance Between the Deep State and Nonprofit Groups

You may be shocked to learn that the nonprofit sector is one of the most powerful promoters, supporters and enablers of the Deep State.

Many people mistakenly believe that conservative nonprofits are more heavily funded than progressive nonprofits. They believe that conservative organizations run on money donated by wealthy, politically conservative benefactors, while progressive nonprofits have less funding.

Here's the reality: Progressive nonprofits, groups and foundations are richly supported with billions – not millions – of dollars. Using this funding, they successfully advance and promote their own radical agenda in our government and culture.

Digging into their rich coffers — funded by corporations, unions and ideologically minded millionaire and billionaire donors — these organizations seek to:

- Sway government policy and protect Deep State interests through political activism

- Undermine individual liberty

- Advance socialism and attack business and the free market

- Manipulate public opinion, sometimes generating mass hysteria

- Advance dangerous social engineering
- Resist and demonize anyone who disagrees with their dangerous ideology

These nonprofits vary widely in purpose. Some of them promote radical environmentalism built on dubious scientific claims. Others push a transgender ideology, or fund mass abortions. Still others fight to impose a socialist healthcare system on America or more government control over the lives of the individual.

They are all forces of political, social and economic influence and deceit that have a direct impact on you and your family.

Here's what you need to know about these foundations, funded and fueled by the Deep State:

1) They're rich – very rich.

One of the biggest lies circulated by the Deep State politicians and media is that politically conservative foundations receive far more funding than liberal foundations, specifically from the Koch brothers. The Kochs are businessmen that have helped fund conservative and libertarian organizations.

Here's the truth: The Koch Family Foundations haven't even been listed in the top 100 foundations for giving – or in the Top 100 foundations in terms of assets.

But they are totally demonized by the Deep State for influencing politics. At the same time, progressive-leaning groups are praised for supporting the "public interest."

In reality, Deep State foundations have funding

that exceeds conservative foundations' funding 10 times over. There are 115 progressive nonprofits in the country with assets exceeding $100 billion. On the other hand, conservative nonprofits have about $10 billion.[1]

These radically progressive foundations receive funding from:

- Wealthy donors and founders — like Nazi collaborator and billionaire George Soros, who gives billions to radical causes and groups that support socialism and other progressive ideologies.

- Socialist, progressive groups such as unions — that gave more than $1.1 billion (from 2010 to 2016) to radical nonprofit groups such as Planned Parenthood ($805,100) and The Center for American Progress ($6,279,591), which advocates a Deep State ideological agenda.[2]

- Corporations such as Google, Apple, Starbucks, Bank of America, Wells Fargo and Facebook, who support progressive causes with major funding and influence.

Rather than funnel their money directly to the poor, some extremely wealthy individuals give money to these tax-exempt foundations in order to obtain tax deductions. The recipients then turn around and use the money for political advocacy.

One of the most powerful Deep State nonprofits is the Ford Foundation. The Ford Foundation has an endowment of more than $12 billion.[3] They use their great wealth to support a socialist, anti-capitalist and anti-business agenda that is radically progressive. Here's a rundown of just a few of their outrageous activities:

- Has given up to $100 million over a six-year period to organizations backing Black Lives Matter, the anti-police movement aimed at social engineering in this country.[4]

- Made a multi-million-dollar contribution to The Mexican American Legal Defense Fund. They poured $25 million into this radical group that promotes citizen rights for illegal aliens.[5]

- Helped create the American Civil Liberties Union (ACLU), with donations of more than $14 million.[6] The ACLU is a dangerous army of lawyers that, among other things, promotes voter fraud by claiming that Voter ID is racist.

Other radically leftist foundations include: The Pew Charitable Trusts, which funds politically motivated "research" to support a progressive worldview, worth $4 billion + , and billionaire George Soros' Open Society Foundations, which seeks to advance George Soros' global socialist political agenda, worth over $18 billion + .[7,8]

Although these organizations wield enormous influence over politics and policy in the United States, they aren't judged to be "political" by the IRS. They remain accountable to no one when engaged in their massive spending. This results in a twisted distortion of our democracy that robs you of your voice in the political process.

2) They're advancing a progressive agenda.

Deep State foundations use their billions of dollars to fund and advance a dangerous, socialist agenda across the nation.

Deep State funding goes to:

- Smaller nonprofits with similar ideologies
- Biased research that supports the claims of the progressive Left
- Political lobbying to ensure their ideology is enacted into law or added to regulations
- Media and community-organizing agitation groups
- Organizing protests and violence

Left-leaning non-profits use their large assets to advance their radical causes. These include:

- **Socialism.** Deep State ideology supporters seek to promote this dangerous economic system that suppresses innovation, freedom and robust competition. Healthcare foundations like the California Endowment promote socialized healthcare by funding projects that push Obamacare. The Deep State promotes the radical and destructive policy of single-payer healthcare. This system causes fatal wait times and ultimately, millions of deaths that could be prevented.

- **Abortion.** Planned Parenthood is one of the Deep State's most vile, aggressive and politicized nonprofits. They fund the genocide of unborn human babies…and sell their body parts. There are multiple other foundations that promote abortion in America, including the Center for Reproductive Rights.

- **Radical environmentalism.** Organizations like Greenpeace USA, the SierraClub and the National Wildlife Federation advance a radical environmental agenda that is anti-free market and anti-business. Their "evidence" for impending environmental disaster is based on dubious scientific claims.

– **Transgenderism is accepted and even encouraged in our schools, in public and in the military by the Deep State.** The Ford Foundation funds LGBT groups with millions of dollars to advance the acceptance of transgenderism. And the Gill Foundation, founded by software business executive Tim Gill, invests hundreds of millions in nonprofits that support the LGBT cause.

These are just a few of the many issues and tax-free organizations that are important to heavily funded Deep State foundations. And these are the values that they fight tooth and nail to impose on every segment of society.

3) They're pushing a radicalized ideology of "resistance."

When you see the slogan "RESIST" on marketing materials or merchandise of a nonprofit, you know the Deep State is behind it.

"RESIST" is a favorite slogan of the Deep State and radical Left, which seek to **resist:**

- The Trump administration, and every reform and change the President wants to make

- Any individual or organization who disagrees with or opposes the Deep State's own value system, ideology and power centers

- The voice of millions of Americans who value individual freedom, family, religious liberty and their constitutional rights

- Anyone who would stop the growth and expansion of the bureaucracy and big government

4) They're attempting to get radicals and activists nominated to the federal judiciary and the U.S. Department of Justice.

As you learned in Chapter Six, judicial activists help to expand Deep State ideology by unconstitutionally legislating their extreme progressive agenda from the bench.

Deep State foundations make every effort to influence judicial selection in this nation. They partner with judicial activists and their dangerous ideology to undermine the supposedly nonpartisan process of judicial selection.

One of the most powerful Deep State-driven groups responsible for supporting judicial activists is the Alliance for Justice (AFJ).

The AFJ is a collaboration of more than 100 socialist/progressive organizations. These organizations are sharply focused on legal issues, with members comprised of radical environmentalist groups, abortion groups and politicized labor unions.

Some of the AFJ's largest donors include The Susan Thompson Buffet Foundation, which has given $1.81 million; Soros' Open Society Foundations, which has given $1.6 million; and the Ford Foundation, which has given $3.36 million.[9]

Using this significant funding, the AFJ advances judicial activism throughout the United States. They work to support judges who will drive their ideological agenda by legislating from the bench.

The AFJ's most infamous project is called "The Judicial Selection Project." This movement has turned the nominations of federal judges into a one-party process that is a dangerous assault on the Constitution.

In the 1980s, the Judicial Selection Project began an all-out attack on President Ronald Reagan's appointees to the federal courts by slandering their characters and qualifications.

Their attacks included the horrific and unjust accusations on Supreme Court nominee Judge Robert Bork. These accusations included allegations that Bork would "close the door to the courts for the poor and the powerless" and that "writers and artists would be censored at the whim of government."[10]

Of course, the accusations were completely untrue and unfounded. Bork had been rated "exceptionally well-qualified" just five years earlier. But the Judicial Selection Project's mudslinging worked, and Judge Bork was not confirmed to the high court.[11]

In many ways, the Alliance for Justice and other radical organizations have succeeded in politicizing the process by which federal judicial nominees are approved.

5) They're creating hysteria.

To manipulate public opinion and influence legislation, the Deep State generates hysteria.

One way that Deep State foundations have created a frenzy around political issues is to pay for "experts" to confirm their dubious claims and support pressure groups that are "calling for reform."[12]

The Pew Trusts — a Deep State nonprofit that aims to influence public policy with progressive ideology

— used this devious tactic in their effort to change the way campaigns are financed in this country. They and others distorted this issue in testimony before the Senate and the House in a vain attempt to get them to vote for bad legislation.

Between 1994 and 2004, the Pew Trusts and others spent approximately $140 million to lobby for campaign finance laws to benefit progressive Democrats. Out of $140 million, $123 million came from eight radically progressive foundations.[13]

Another powerful strategy that Deep State foundations use to manipulate public opinion and policy is to generate biased, distorted "research" that affirms their ideology.

Before Elizabeth Warren entered the political scene, she conducted "research" on medical bankruptcy that supported a socialized healthcare system. The research was not funded by Harvard Law School, where she worked as a professor. It was funded by massive grants from the radically leftist Robert Wood Johnson Foundation. In order to evade the strict standards that Harvard Law School requires in scientific research, the study was conducted through the Cambridge Medical Care Foundation (CMCF).

CMCF was directed by a socialist activist whose goal was to create "social change" through dubious research, like that used by Warren.[14]

In the end, Warren's "research" could never have passed peer review under the scrutiny of Harvard Law School's process. But it achieved its aim, thrusting her into the political spotlight and giving her falsified credibility (Warren also falsely claimed to be a member of the Cherokee Nation to support her own political aims).

Remember, the Deep State cares about expanding its own power and influence, not about acting with integrity and transparency.

Another example of hysterical rabble-rousing from Deep State foundations is their use of dubious or junk science to support extreme environmentalism.

The Natural Resources Defense Council (NRDC) is a nonprofit group that uses hysteria to generate publicity — and funding.

Here are a few examples of the manipulative strategies that the NRDC has used to advance their radical ideology:

- Using unreliable scientific claims to cause fear about the safety of chemicals used in food production, such as the use of the pesticide Alar in the apple industry. The NRDC blamed Alar for 5,300 cases of cancer in children, causing apples to be pulled off the shelves and apple growers to lose more than $250 million. The entire campaign was later proved to be a completely fake money-making scheme that produced $700,000 for the NRDC.[15]

- Partnering with the Environmental Protection Agency in "Sue and Settle" lawsuits to produce stricter regulations with less interference. The NRDC colludes with this inefficient government agency by suing the agency and then accepting hefty settlements ... all funded by your tax dollars.

- Reporting on a "swordfish shortage" to persuade the government to issue stricter regulations, hindering the fishing business. The campaign backing the swordfish shortage was called "flawed to the core" by the U.S.

Fish and Wildlife Service, and swordfish were reported "not...endangered" by the director of the Highly Migratory Species Division of the National Marine Fisheries Service.[16] As a result of their disinformation, many U.S. fishermen lost their jobs, but the NRDC generated publicity, money and more government regulations with their deceitful actions.

It's no surprise that the NRDC was founded with a $400,000 grant from the Ford Foundation. It also continues to receive millions from other liberal organizations, including George Soros' Open Society Foundations, Institute, which donated more than $2.2 million in the past decade, and the William and Flora Hewlett Foundation, which donated over $4.7 million in the past decade.[17]

Today, the NRDC has assets of more than $180 million.[18]

In creating the illusion of public hysteria over political issues, Deep State foundations help convince lawmakers and the general public to believe their fake science and incredibly biased viewpoint.

6) They're spreading hate and slander.

One of the most effective ways that the Deep State promotes its agenda of hate is to slander or libel anyone who disagrees with their ideology. They will call the Deep State's opponents "bigoted," "racist" and "hateful"....among other things.

It's disturbing, but their approach to spreading hate is calculated and methodical.

The Southern Poverty Law Center (SPLC) is a nonprofit that specializes in legal advocacy. But its current foundations lie in its morally corrupt and libelous "hate map."

The SPLC labels anyone who disagrees with their progressive ideology – including Conservative, Libertarian and Christian organizations – as "hate groups." They show hate groups on their "hate map" and then feed this deceptive garbage to the media, who often treat the SPLC as an unbiased source of truth.

The SPLC's "hate map" groups together genuinely hateful organizations – such as KKK groups or Nazis – with groups that promote family values and civil rights for Christians, such as the Family Research Alliance and the Pacific Justice Institute.

The SPLC has viciously attacked individuals such as Franklin Graham – missionary, evangelist, founder of Samaritan's Purse and son of the late Dr. Billy Graham; David Horowitz – conservative speaker, author and advocate for freedom and liberty; and Dennis Prager – conservative radio talk-show host and defender of family values.

Media outlets such as CBS, ABC, NBC, MSNBC and CNN use these labels as fodder for their Deep State-inspired news stories. And, the SPLC continues to try to destroy the reputations and credibility of Conservative and Christian groups.

7) They're being funded deceptively.

In the 1990s, many nonprofit healthcare plans became for-profit healthcare plans. In the process, they were required to establish separate "philanthropic" foundations with their assets.

The result was the establishment of multiple foundations, financed with billions of dollars between

1984 and 2006.

Today, there are healthcare foundations in 15 states and the District of Columbia that receive generous funding from liberal organizations and foundations. These foundations also provide additional sources of revenue for for-profit healthcare plans.

The California Endowment is one of the largest and most powerful of these foundations. In fact, it's one of the richest foundations in the United States, with more than $3.5 billion in assets.[19]

Using their hefty funding, the California Endowment supports a number of radical causes. For example, they issue grants for the Families U.S.A Foundation, which promotes Obamacare. They also pay for marketing efforts for the anti-police, anarchic Black Lives Matter radicals.

These foundations have completely altered the healthcare landscape and opened the door for corruption and financial fraud.

Progressive nonprofit foundations are some of the most powerful actors in promoting the Deep State.

By colluding with:

- Rich progressive ideologues
- Judicial activists
- Government bureaucrats
- Other agents of resistance to true progress in our nation

… these nonprofit groups are successfully advancing their dangerous agenda. This agenda attacks value systems, steals our tax dollars and mocks and seeks to destroy our core principles of freedom, family and constitutional rights.

CHAPTER 10

The Deep State's Dirty Little Secret: Organizing for Action (OFA)

Few Americans know how:

- Organized
- Well-financed
- Marketing and advertising savvy
- Technologically cutting edge...

The progressive Left is.

Because of this, they are a powerful force.

Unfortunately, most Conservative, Christian, and Libertarian groups are disorganized, lacking in funding, and inept at marketing and technology.

Most Conservative groups advertise, market, and promote as if it's 2000.

On the other hand, progressives mobilize as if it's 2022.

And they are the allies and defenders of the Deep State.

One under-the-radar group that echoes Deep State resistance ... advocates for bigger bureaucracy ... and is aggressive in mobilizing support is Organizing for Action (OFA).

Fewer know how powerful this organization is in transforming our politics and government infrastructure into a Deep State tool.

Less understood or even known, however, are the power and reality of the system behind this calculated assault on our values and our rights.

As you've discovered in the previous chapters, there is a systemic attack on freedom and our constitutional rights in this nation, much of it advanced by entrenched government employees ... the bloated bureaucracy ... politicization within our government agencies ... and collusion among nonprofits, wealthy progressive ideologues and radical judicial activists.

It's a decentralized network with a united purpose of expanding government and opposing anything that would slow, halt, or remove its progressive agenda. There's no one single "ringleader" in the Deep State, but an intentional, widespread agenda.

That being said, Organizing for Action is a "power player" in the Deep State that acts as a centralized, highly organized network to:

- Deliberately attack anything that would undo the government's bureaucratic policies remaining from the Obama administration
- Forcefully resist anyone who disagrees with its policies in the Trump administration
- Promote a socialist agenda in lawmaking, public opinion and culture

What if I told you that this "power player" has actually prepared for years to advance calculated efforts of socializing and collectivizing ... and resistance to opponents?

...that they recruit and train millennial disciples to aggressively and systematically promote their dangerous ideology?

...that they are equipped with the most advanced resources in marketing and technology to successfully achieve their agenda?

This organization is perhaps more dangerous to

freedom than any other well-known organization.

Organizing For Action (OFA) is one of the Deep State's most powerful cabals for transforming our society — for the worse!

In the following pages, you'll discover the secretive tactics this group of roughly 30,000 liberal ideologues is using to manipulate the Millennial Generation and ensure that their political and social aims are met – at the expense of freedom and economic growth.[1]

Secret #1: OFA seeks to preserve the political agenda of Barack Obama, long after he has stepped out of the Oval Office.

Organizing for Action's primary aim is to preserve the political agenda of former President Barak Obama – at any cost.

Originally called "Organizing for America" and founded after Obama's election in 2008, the organization was also the community-organizing arm of Obama's second presidential campaign, in 2012.

It grew from the idea of taking community activists and mobilization to win local elections to using technology and the internet to win elections and transform politics and culture.

Organizing for Action relaunched its efforts when Trump was elected President, in preparation for resisting his reforms at all costs and maintaining or expanding Obama's ideologically progressive agenda and to resist and obstruct change or challenge to the Deep State from the Trump administration.

Of the movement, Michelle Obama said that the OFA would help Obama followers "finish what we started and truly make that change we believe in." In other words, to maintain her husband's executive authority after it has been legally terminated.[2]

To prepare for this "soft coup," the OFA geared up with a massive new hiring and marketing strategy to launch an assault on Trump's agenda.

The original goal of the OFA was to get President Obama elected ... then re-elected.

It's the first organization in American history where a President set up an independent political organization to be his own political tool.

The corrupt goal of OFA is to ensure a sort of "shadow presidency," where the agenda of former President Obama is promoted and everything else is actively opposed.

Through grassroots activism, "town halls," brilliant marketing and heavy recruitment, OFA works to promote:

- Obamacare's existence and growth
- Radical environmentalism
- Uncontrolled and unlimited immigration
- An LGBT agenda to force acceptance, not tolerance
- Big Government expansion and socialism
- More deceitful and dangerous progressive ideology

...in almost every city and state in America.

When Trump was elected President, the organization was re-energized to expand its reach into new areas of influence, including increased gun control and so-called man-made climate change.

From candidate recruitment and training, to community activism to massive data collection and mobilization, the OFA is an under-the-radar power player.

Secret #2: OFA is extremely well-funded.

OFA is officially a nonprofit 501 (c)4, but like the Deep State nonprofits described in Chapter Nine, it's richly funded, with amazing ability to advance its ideological agenda.

OFA made public that it raised $40 million in 2013 but has not publicly released any fundraising information on its finances.[3] Since their thousands of volunteers aren't paid, they have a massive budget for their top-level staff and operating costs.

Few Conservative or Libertarian groups can come close to such money.

From whom does Organizing for Action receive its funding?

Let's take a look at some of their billionaire and millionaire donors:

- David Shaw, the founder of a hedge-fund company, is known as "the most intriguing and mysterious force on Wall Street."[4] Shaw has donated $1 million to OFA.[5]

- Amy Goldman Fowler, a real estate heiress, has given $750,000 to OFA.[6]

- Ryan Smith, a venture capitalist whose source of funding is unknown, has given $351,260 to OFA.[7]

- And the list goes on...including donors like San Francisco-based philanthropists John and Marcia Goldman ($325,000) and Barbara Grasseschi and Anthony Crabb ($285,000) who have also contributed generously to support same-sex marriage.[8]

But OFA doesn't just rely on massive contributions from wealthy, ideologically motivated donors.

Using strategic email and digital marketing, they raise continuous donations from hundreds of thousands of supporters on the database with pleas to "become an OFA Champion" by making monthly donations.

Secret #3: The OFA prepared for Obama's re-election for an entire year — inside a secretive room called "The Cave."

How did Obama win the presidency a second time?

The year before his 2012 re-election campaign, Obama's approval rating dropped to an all-time low — less than 40 percent in August 2011.[9]

When the 2010 election saw a Republican victory at the polls, panic set in. President Obama was shocked and discouraged by the Tea Party uprising.

But in 2012, Obama was re-elected as President of the United States largely as the result of the brilliant marketing strategy and tactics of OFA.

While Obama's agenda did not have the best interests of the American people at heart, and while many people disagreed with his policies, OFA was at the core of Obama's re-election campaign, and had a powerful advantage: "The Cave."

"The Cave" was the name of the windowless room where 50 data analysts from OFA were gathered in secret, working tirelessly to brainwash and control voters with the most advanced marketing machine.

OFA's staff included 50 top-level strategists and data analysts from Silicon Valley, Fortune 500 companies and academia, strategically recruited to develop perhaps the most sophisticated political marketing campaign of all time.

With a staff that included a high-energy particle physicist, a software engineer from Pixar and digital specialist from Twitter, they used sophisticated analytics to constantly improve their marketing efforts and strategically target their ideal audience of voters. In fact, every night they ran 66,000 simulations to see which political candidate was winning.[10]

It was a marketing machine that used the most advanced strategies and tactics.

It transformed modern politics.

All of a sudden, consultants with old school politics were out.

And targeted, digital data was in.

Using that information, they honed in on the states where Obama was losing, and targeted tens of thousands of new voters with their brilliant marketing strategies to capture the vote.

Mitt Romney's campaign had similar funding, but his data staff had only four people, outnumbered by more than ten-to-one by "The Cave."

Not only that, but Romney's marketing strategy and output were paltry compared to Obama's high-level marketing tactics birthed in "The Cave":

- Obama spent $47 million on Facebook advertising; Romney spent $4.7 million.
- Obama sent 16 million emails; Romney sent 3 million emails.
- Obama's videos received 133 million views; Romney's videos received 1 million views.

- 600,000 commercials aired in support of the Obama campaign; 250,000 commercials aired in support of the Romney campaign.

- Finally, while Obama's campaign organization had 4,000 employees, 12,700 field staff, 8,000 neighborhood team leaders, and 32,000 highly trained volunteers, Romney's organization had only 284 field offices and 61 key staff.

Romney's marketing efforts were completely dwarfed by the brilliant innovation and relentless determination of "The Cave" ... and in the end, Obama won the election.

Let me tell you about the "test-run" for Obama's decisive victory ... and how the OFA personally targeted my own political campaign in 2011:

When Congresswoman Jane Harman resigned from Congress in 2011, some people suggested I run for Congress. I decided to enter the race, although I was coming up against some very powerful people, including the mayor of Redondo Beach, City Councilman of Hermosa Beach, the Secretary of State, and Los Angeles Councilwoman Janice Hahn of the powerful Hahn family dynasty in California.

In this race, I had zero name recognition. However, I was able to mobilize people in the district, especially Christians, to get out the vote. When I beat Debra Bowen, Secretary of State, the results sent shock waves, not only through California, but nationwide. Suddenly, I was on national television. Suddenly, major press stations were talking about how a safe democratic district in California was about ready to be won by a "Tea Party" Conservative-Libertarian.

My opponents began receiving a massive amount of money and support from the Clintons, Nancy Pelosi, and the Democratic Establishment. On the surface, we were being outspent 3:1, but something else was happening — something strange that couldn't be explained by traditional consultants. They told me, "Don't worry about it."

Wherever I went, whether it be church, to the market, or to a restaurant, people would come up to me and tell me "I got this call." If they were gun rights advocates, they would get a call about gun rights. If they were for or against abortion, they got a call about abortion. The callers would spend 10-15 minutes using the recipient's personal details to manipulate their opinion of me.

These phone calls were being made by OFA volunteers who had the personal data and profiles of constituents in my district ... and used this valuable information to try to destroy my credibility with potential voters and advance the position of my opponent.

Even so, I came close to winning, shocking everybody on election day.

However, what nobody knew was reported in the next day in the *L.A. Times*:

"...Obama campaign manager Jim Messina discussed the transition of Organizing for America from a movement that supported the president's agenda in the first half of his term to one working now toward helping him secure a second term.

*One aspect of that is a summer organizer program, which accepted 1,500 supporters from a field of nearly 12,000 applicants nationwide to begin the effort. **Some of that grass-roots army was deployed on behalf of Janice Hahn in the special election in the 36th District, which amounted to a test run.***

According to a Democratic official, Organizing for America's California operation organized 41 phone banks during the get-out-the-vote phase, 33 of which were run by volunteers. All told, the official estimates, volunteers worked 1,509 hours making calls on Hahn's behalf. On election day, 394 people signed up through the group to work on phone bank and canvass events.

In a low-turnout race in a district suffering voter fatigue, that effort was crucial, the Hahn campaign said.

The Democratic Congressional Campaign Committee and the California Democratic Party also assisted Hahn's campaign, making nearly 410,000 live voter calls along with organizing groups in the last 20 days of the campaign."[11]

The OFA's special "test-run" had been performed on my own campaign — and cost me victory.

I could not successfully defeat a campaign that had made hundreds of thousands of phone calls, and must have relied on potentially millions of dollars of undisclosed funding.

This campaign had also become the test campaign for the 2012 election that devastated Romney.

By coordinating the most advanced marketing technology, special favors from Facebook, and advanced profiling of data with a "Get out the Vote" campaign, my opponents had developed a powerful machine. This strategy was undefeatable, unless you tried to do it yourself.

What Obama did in the 2011 special election and eventually for his own campaign transformed politics from a consultant class into the best of marketing, the best of technology and the best of "getting out the vote" merged together.

Secret #4: The OFA uses a special "resistance manual" to set the stage for activists to effectively resist any of Trump's reforms.

One of the OFA's key strategies is to indoctrinate "normal" Americans to goad lawmakers to resist all of Trump's reforms, including those relating to illegal immigration, tax cuts and jobs.

They were able to indoctrinate people by partnering with another resistance movement, known as Indivisible, and their secretive, highly strategic guide called "Indivisible, A Practical Guide for Resisting the Trump Agenda." Indivisible trains Americans to stop Trump's agenda using principles gleaned, ironically, from the Tea Party movement.

The guide encourages readers to use the following tactics, among others, to manipulate members of Congress:

- Opposition is the unifying factor. Don't focus on the creation of new law. Focus on saying NO to Trump.

- Sap energy away from Trump's reforms using distraction and hysteria in Town Halls, public events and angry letters.

- Present yourself as a "representative" of the people to manipulate members of Congress into thinking your ideology is the dominant one.

- Scare Representatives into refusing to support Trump's changes. Take advantage of their single-minded focus on re-election to make them feel afraid to disagree with you.

- Start your own ideological group, if necessary, and recruit others to join the "resistance" movement.

Indivisible has become the primary guide of the OFA and much of the Deep State movement. Using firm directives and calls to action, the book prepares Deep State style-resistance at the grassroots level, transforming ordinary Americans into manipulative ideologues.

Secret #5: OFA is a master recruiter and marketer.

OFA spreads its Deep State message of resistance to change through recruitment and marketing.

OFA seeks to recruit and mobilize millennials into a movement that is supposedly spreading a message of "hope." But in reality, OFA and its pawns are expanding a campaign of ideological manipulation that wars against the foundations of our nation.

OFA preys on young, impressionable college students with limited knowledge of politics, and recruits them into their army of ideologues. In the 2012 presidential election, thousands of volunteers made tens of thousands of phone calls and knocked on thousands of doors to vote for Obama.

Their efforts were rewarded. More than two out of three voters aged 18-29 voted for Obama.[12] In swing states, this proved to be decisive for victory.

And OFA continues to heavily recruit individuals for its ideological army, partially through ingenious marketing tactics.

When you sign up for the OFA email list – pitched as joining a movement for "lasting change" (read: installment of a permanent political elite) – you immediately begin to receive an onslaught of emails.

Written with arrogant, self-righteous anger, the emails are sent from a variety of senders that have encouraged recipients to:

- Resist Trump's Tax Reform Bill, with a button to call a senator
- Share social media graphics that promote the DREAM Act
- Apply to be an OFA activist, to actively oppose gun control, for example
- Donate cash to help defeat Repeal and Replace of Obamacare

Thousands of people respond to these persuasive emails and call their local politicians, hysterical about Trump's reforms, because they've been fed a slanted perspective and misinformation from OFA.

This is exactly OFA's aim: To invoke hysteria in the people, and fear in the politicians.

A House Representative or State Senator who is flooded with phone calls and emails from concerned constituents about a specific issue is going to panic. They're going to think their position is at risk, and they're going to resist the reforms that OFA is working so feverishly against.

OFA also uses data-profiling, an advanced marketing technique that gives them the ability to target select populations of people they would like "on their side."

For example, OFA targets charter-school teachers to recruit them into unions. Using their brilliant email marketing techniques and making phone calls, they will contact this specific audience until they say they will do what they want.

The persistent marketing of arrogant opposition to

downsize, create efficiency, and other reforms is an insidious and disturbingly effective tactic for promoting the Deep State's resistance message.

The Trump administration, Conservative values and any plan for reform and change are faced with an organized resistance that is unheard of and unprecedented in politics.

Using brilliant strategy and political manipulation, OFA has achieved its political aims and imposed radical social engineering across the nation.

Organizing for Action is truly the ultimate arm of the sinister Deep State.

It's a calculated effort to manipulate the political process and to resist anyone who disagrees with its own radicalized belief system.

CHAPTER 11

Voter Fraud: Earning the Deep State More Votes, More Power … While Trampling on Your Rights and Suppressing Your Voice as a Citizen

The Deep State hates light and truth.

Government ineptitude, corruption, incompetence… are all hidden at any cost.

No government bureaucrat wants the truth to expose problems or corruption.

And that's the case with elected or unelected government officials hiding and denying the existence of voter fraud in America.

Voter fraud attacks your rights as a U.S. citizen… undermines your voice with millions of false votes… and advances the agenda and ideology of the Deep State.

Voter fraud:

- Is facilitated and even encouraged by Deep State ideologues

- Increases the likelihood that political candidates who participate in the Deep State will be elected

- Crushes your rights and silences your voice as a participant in the democratic process

The abundant evidence of voter fraud nationwide is shocking, but Deep State ideologues like to spread the lie that voter fraud is a myth.

That's because they know that the corruption of one of our core foundational political processes in a Constitutional Republic will help them advance their goals of:

- Government/bureaucratic expansion and growth

- Greater control over the lives of the individual

- Preventing progress and change if they are at odds with collectivism and socialism

In the following pages, you'll learn more about the shocking evidence of voter fraud in this nation…and how the Deep State is using this attack on individual rights and corruption of a political process for their own benefit.

FALSE: Voter fraud doesn't exist.

The overwhelming evidence of voter fraud in the United States will shock you — but Deep State politicians and bureaucrats don't want you to know about it.

A 2012 Pew Study showed that 24 million voter registrations in the United States were inaccurate, out-of-date or duplicate.[1] And, in 2017, another study found that in 24 states, there were 248 counties where the number of registered voters exceeded the number of eligible voters.[2]

A shocking example is the state of California, where there are 11 counties with more registered voters than eligible voters. In San Diego, the number of registered voters is 138% of eligible voters; in Los Angeles it is 112% and in San Francisco, it is 114%[3]

The Deep State, of course, doesn't want you to know the truth — that voter fraud is an all-too-real threat to our individual freedom and to our constitutional right as American citizens to elect our own leaders.

Collusion between Deep State bureaucrats, politicians and the media have all propagated the myth that voter fraud doesn't exist.

Politicians and bureaucrats — including state and local level officials — refuse to investigate.

The media mock the idea of investigating voter fraud.

But what do they have to fear in investigating?

The evidence is clear. And as you'll see in the following pages, voter fraud is committed by illegal aliens, dead people, duplicate voters and felons... corrupting American elections and stealing your vote.

TRUE: Voter fraud is disturbingly easy to commit.

Deep State ideologues have made the voter registration process so easy and inept that it's actually easy to commit voter fraud.

I was curious to see how easy it is to register as a "fake person" in the state of California, so I registered online under a false name to see how far I could get in the voting process.

Keep in mind, I only provided a name, date of birth, ethnicity, party preference, and state of birth. I did not falsify a social security number or driver's license number.

Once I registered, I immediately received paperwork asking for further information. But before I could provide it, I received a ballot in the mail (Of course, I didn't use this ballot to vote).

The process was disturbingly simple — and proved

that anyone could vote under a false name. There was no need for proof of who I was, or proof of my citizenship. Just a simple form and a two- or three-step online process.

TRUE: An estimated 2 million illegal aliens could be registered to vote in the United States — and are choosing who will run our country.

The United States was founded on the principle that we as a people have the right to choose who governs us. This is a right and a responsibility we enjoy as U.S. citizens, not given to anyone who enters the country illegally.

But according to the National Hispanic Survey, there are 2 million illegal aliens registered to vote in this country.[4] And in another study confirming the findings, in a random sample of 800 Hispanic voters, 13% admitted they were not citizens.[5]

That means at least 2 million noncitizens have the power to sabotage and steal our elections by voting illegally...choose who runs our cities, states and nation...and influence the most important legislation in America.

Evidence for massive numbers of noncitizens voting illegally in U.S. elections has been uncovered in Kansas, Maryland, Pennsylvania, California, Virginia and other states.

In fact, in the swing state of Virginia, one study showed that there are more than 5,000 noncitizens who are registered to vote ... and who are actively casting their ballots.[6]

When President Trump tried to investigate this type of voter fraud with his Commission on Election Integrity, Deep State politicians and bureaucrats were furious and refused to comply with the commission's requests for voter-roll information.

California Secretary of State Alex Padilla even called the commission a "fraud" and a "sham"[7] — knowing that exposure of such critical information would reveal voter fraud that keeps Democrat politicians like him in power.

TRUE: Illegal aliens are far more likely to vote for someone who will promise to give them money and other government benefits at the expense of hard-working American citizens.

Deep State politicians will protect the "rights" of illegal aliens because they know that it will earn them more votes. They do not want to protect our borders, refuse to require Voter ID and love to legislate simple, automated registration (like same-day registration) because they know these measures will only increase the noncitizen vote.

Their goal is not to uphold constitutional principles. Their goal is to increase their power.

And noncitizens invariably help Deep State ideologues to win — and to advance their political agendas. Take a look at the following examples:

– In the 2008 election between Barak Obama and John McCain, an estimated 6.4% of noncitizens voted.[8] And noncitizens would have most likely voted for Obama because he promised to help them with money and government handouts.

– During the Obama administration, noncitizen votes helped pass Obamacare, by electing Minnesota's extreme progressive and alleged sexual predator Al Franken to the U.S. Senate in 2008…giving Senate Democrats the critical

60th vote needed to overcome filibusters against their disastrous socialist healthcare system.

– In the 2016 election, an estimated 800,000 noncitizens voted. Again, roughly 81% of them would have voted for Hillary Clinton.[9] In fact, she actually initiated a program to create a "voter registration army" — with the help of illegal aliens — that recruited other noncitizens into the election process.

It's probable that illegal aliens have significantly affected the outcome in local, state, congressional, and even elections for the U.S.—potentially corrupting the integrity of the electoral college itself.

TRUE: Dead voters, duplicate voters and felons are also casting ballots.

Voter fraud isn't limited to the millions of illegal immigrants who have been illegally registered to vote. They are openly casting their ballots right under the noses of our state and local authorities.

Voter fraud also exists in millions of votes cast by dead people, duplicate voters and felons.

Dead people continue to vote…5, 10, or 20 years after they've died.

It's shocking, but a lot of dead people, many of them dead for decades, are still "voting." Their voter registrations are alive and well, and someone will pick up their registration and vote for them.

Take a look at the following examples:

– An illegal immigrant living in Sacramento, California used a dead man's identity for 25 years to cast his ballot in multiple elections.

- A student from James Madison University, in Virginia, was put in jail for attempting to vote using 18 falsified registration forms, many using the names of the dead. The student worked for "Harrisonburg Votes," a Democrat front group that told him to "register as many voters as possible and report them to Democratic headquarters in Harrisonburg."

- An investigative reporter in Los Angeles found 265 dead voters in Southern California by comparing millions of voting records from the California Secretary of State with records from the U.S. Social Security database. These dead voters included John Cenkner, who died in 2003, but who voted almost every year after that until 2010. Like many of the dead voters, Cenkner was a registered Democrat.

"Voting from beyond the grave" sounds like a scary movie...but it's all too real...and votes from the deceased destroy your rights and steal your vote in the election process.

One voter...casting two votes.

Duplicate votes are a massive problem all over the nation, as people use absentee ballots or double-registrations to vote in multiple states.

I still receive absentee ballots in California for my kids living of state, who are also registered in their new home states. And this is all too common — as voter registration rolls are completely neglected, leaving room for fraud.

In fact, more than 7 million people are registered to vote in two different states.[10] This data was compiled after a crosscheck of 28 states, meaning the number is potentially twice as high nationwide — more than

14 million duplicate voters in two states.

In swing states where the vote is critical, this could easily make the difference in deciding who is elected as Senator, member of Congress or President of the United States.

For example, there are 95,000 voters in New Hampshire who are registered in two states – with 40,000 voters registered to vote in both New Hampshire and Massachusetts — meaning fraudulent voters might vote in Massachusetts in the morning, and New Hampshire in the afternoon, illegally doubling the power of their votes.[11]

In Massachusetts, where political sentiment and Deep State ideology run high, it is almost certain that this affected the 2016 election. Hillary Clinton won New Hampshire by fewer than 3,000 votes out of more than 700,000.[12]

Duplicate votes have been uncovered again and again; but if those votes work to the advantage of Democrat politicians or officials who have a Deep State ideology, they will refuse to take steps to stop or prosecute illegal voting behavior.

Voting from behind bars.

In most states, convicted felons lose the right to vote. When they commit a felony, they are no longer allowed to vote or hold office.

But in some states, convicted criminals are still voting — receiving ballots in jail and casting their votes from behind bars.

In Minnesota, one group found that 1,099 felons had voted in the race between Al Franken and Norm Coleman.[13]

Or take the example of Deszi Marquis Hayes, who

was serving a nine-month sentence when he voted in the 2016 election. Hayes received a mail-in ballot in the Indian River County jail and cast his vote — while locked up for a felony traffic conviction.

In Florida, Democrat chief election official Brenda Snipes admitted that felons have been allowed to vote in Broward County. In fact, there were more voters registered on Broward voter rolls than there were eligible voters.

The evidence of convicted felons voting is overwhelming, but Deep State politicians want to facilitate voter fraud so that thugs who have committed heinous crimes get to choose the people who make the laws and manage our government.

TRUE: Voter fraud has been supported and enabled by Deep State politicians through the "Motor Voter" law in the state of California.

Deep State politicians and bureaucrats in California have supported voter fraud driven by a dangerous ideology that uses loopholes in DMV laws that encourage illegal aliens to vote.

They even passed a law known as the California Motor Voter Act, which automatically sends driver information to state voter-rolls unless the license holder opts out or is not eligible.

This new law — combined with California's 2 million illegal immigrants and notoriously fraudulent voter rolls — all add up to create one chaotic reality:[14] In California, it's easy for voter fraud to happen, for illegals to vote for the politicians who will protect them, and for ideologues to manipulate the vote in their favor.

The California Motor Voter Act makes it nearly

impossible for the state to verify that people are who they claim to be — such as noncitizens claiming to have U.S. citizenship.

Furthermore, because California issues driver's licenses to illegal immigrants, these noncitizens are potentially registered to vote at the same time. All it takes for an illegal alien to register is a dishonest clerk.

I talked about this dangerous reality on Fox News in an interview with Stuart Varney.

Stuart asked me, "Craig, what is voter fraud in California?"

I answered him, and explained: "This is a terrible joke on the United States, because it's going to affect Congress and the Senate races as well as state races, and the electoral college vote in 2020."

I continued, "California politicians wrote into the law that if somebody who was not a citizen registered to vote and voted, they would be held harmless — it doesn't matter if it was an accident or not."

Before Donald Trump was elected President, many in the media were saying: "As California goes, so goes the country."

California is not the only state where illegal aliens can obtain licenses, meaning other states may follow suit. In Colorado, Connecticut, Delaware, Hawaii, Illinois, Maryland, New Mexico, Nevada, Utah, Vermont, Washington and Washington, D.C., illegal aliens can also register to vote with the Department of Motor Vehicles or other agency. This makes it relatively easy in these states for illegal aliens to vote in our elections.

TRUE: President Trump has fought back against voter fraud — but the Deep State resisted repeatedly and refused to comply.

In response to the horrific reality of noncitizen voter fraud, President Trump signed an Executive Order establishing the Presidential Commission on Election Integrity to investigate voter fraud in different states. The committee investigated voter fraud, in part, by requesting voter data from every state.

Deep State politicians and bureaucrats were, of course, furious.

State after state refused to supply the data to the commission, arguing that it would further "voter suppression," a myth promoted by Deep State politicians and bureaucrats who want to give the vote to anyone who will join their ideological army.

At least eight lawsuits have been filed against the Commission, claiming that requests for state voter data violated open-records laws or breached privacy — even though much of this information is on public record.

The lawsuits are used as expensive weapons to stop or slow down measures that would help ensure fair and honest elections that the Deep State doesn't like.

In every case, corrupt Deep State-supported systems are threatened by having the truth come out about election fraud.

President Trump was pressured to shut down the voter fraud Commission because of pushback from states, noncompliance, and lawsuits. But he hasn't surrendered. In fact, he has made a move that will actually increase the crackdown on voter fraud.

The President is now shifting the fight against voter

fraud to the Department of Homeland Security.

This will help reduce or eliminate voter fraud and counteract interference from Deep State ideologues who refuse to publicly acknowledge the widespread existence of illegal voters, duplicate votes, and other forms of fraud.

TRUE: You can help stop voter fraud.

Opposition to the Presidential Commission on Election Integrity was the work of the Deep State, who supports the lie that voter fraud is not a serious and widespread problem.

Voter fraud has the potential to affect an entire election — and the leaders, policy makers, and judges who often exercise the power to make critical decisions about our nation, our individual freedom and our future.

But you can play an important part in fighting this corruption in U.S. elections.

According to the National Conference of State Legislatives, 32% of states have no voter ID requirement, 30% have non-strict, non-photo voter ID laws, 18% have non-strict, photo voter ID laws, 6% have strict, non-photo ID laws, and only 14% have strict photo ID laws.[15]

That needs to change.

- We need to demand strict, photo voter ID laws in every state.
- We need to clean up voter rolls.
- We need to take strong steps that prevent fraud in an age of hacking.

You can help stop voter fraud by speaking up against this injustice and demanding that we put into place laws that will help ensure integrity, transparency and efficiency in our electoral process.

CHAPTER 12

The Media: Giving Voice to the Deep State

For decades, the American people have relied on TV news, newspapers and other forms of journalism to communicate critical information about current events, our politicians, elections and, in general, what's going on in the United States.

Today, most of us also turn to social media like Facebook for news and information about current events.

Regardless of what form it comes in, the business of journalism has been to deliver information to you and your family — to inform and educate you as a citizen, a voter and a taxpayer.

The ideal of journalism is being a champion for truth and transparency.

Sadly, on both the local and national level – and on the internet – that is no longer the case.

The media have become ideological partisans fighting for a progressive agenda to persuade and slant the news in favor of big government and statism.

And, as the Deep State has become increasingly combative in promoting a progressive agenda, the media have become its ally, defender and advocate.

Simply put, "mainstream news" has been in collusion with the Deep State to transform our nation and destroy anyone in its way.

Of this sinister joint venture, former State Department foreign service officer and congressional policy adviser and analyst James George Jatras said,

"American media increasingly have operated uncritically in conjunction with the bipartisan Washington political establishment."[1]

Much of the media no longer even pretend to be objective. They are unapologetically partisan, left-leaning and ideologically driven.

But some are so entrenched in the culture of bias and distortion that they actually think they are objective. I talked with one major political reporter who was convinced he was objective. But 92% of his local TV reporting is biased in favor of a progressive agenda that ignores or ridicules any opposing views.

Colluding with newspapers, reporters, commentators, journalists, and editors, the Deep State has transformed the media into a left-leaning partisan political machine, designed to slander, spread hate and manipulate the American public into subscribing to the "mainstream" media's own progressive beliefs.

And the Deep State doesn't just influence the media. It has taken near-total control of our TV and radio news reporting, newspapers, magazines and online news services.

Take TV:

- Most local TV
- CBS
- NBC
- ABC
- CNN
- MSNBC
- Spanish language networks
- PBS

The media want to control what you think, believe, see and hear — and blindly agree with their own radical progressive ideology.

This highly partisan reality became instantly

apparent with the election of President Trump.

Trump is not the subject of objective reporting. He is the media's target for destruction, half-truths and distortions — relentless, constant, without mercy.

Just look at these three tactics and realities:

#1 Outrageous, Calculated Assault On President Trump

What we've witnessed in the modern media's calculated attack against the presidency of Donald Trump is unprecedented in its blatant partisanship and hostility.

Local and national media present a nonstop assault unprecedented in American history.

Journalists have historically been more left-leaning in their politics...and presidents haven't always been treated objectively by the media.

For example, Ronald Reagan faced an enormous amount of criticism from the media for his tax cuts and strong foreign policy opposition to Communism, then proved them all wrong with his accomplishments.

In fact, his economic policies created a booming economy and more than 20 million new jobs, and his foreign policy brought about the collapse of the Soviet Union.

By contrast, the media had a virtual love affair with President Jimmy Carter's and Barack Obama's domestic and international policies.

But the media's relentless assault on Trump's policies and character marks an historic shift. This is no longer the work of a few journalists or commentators that dislike the president. This is an intentional, vicious effort to take down a President by an organized collusion between:

- Cable television news stations including CBS, NBC, CNN, MSNBC, ABC, PBS and CNBC, who run an endless stream of angry and often hysterical anti-Trump news pieces instead of covering important news and current events.

- Major newspapers including *The New York Times* and *The Washington Post*, who no longer limit "opinions" to the op-ed section, but who propagate anti-Trump bias from the front page to the sports section.

- Internet search engines and powerhouses such as Google, YouTube and Facebook, who censor and discriminate against conservative news and commentary.

- Deep State government bureaucrats and politicians who have an ideologically-driven zeal to expand their power, stop positive change and maintain the status quo.

This twisted relationship is, in part, supported by the progressive ideologues who have founded, funded or purchased major media sources, like Mark Zuckerberg, who started Facebook – quickly becoming America's #1 source for news – or Amazon's Jeff Bezos, who bought *The Washington Post*.

Their objective is not to deliver an unbiased picture of reality to the American public — it's to propagate their radical political viewpoints.

Ignoring reality, honing in on specific statements President Trump has expressed to the point of exhaustion, refusing to acknowledge his accomplishments and painting a picture of a "dictator" or "madman" running our nation have been just a few of the American media's supposedly "unbiased" approaches to reporting about President Trump.

While running as the Republican nominee in the 2016 election, Donald Trump was given a lot of attention by the media. While mocking his politics, they unwittingly helped promote his message and propel him to the lead in the race — and he secured the nomination despite their mockery and hostility.

Then, in a scramble to destroy his chances of winning, TV and cable stations, newspapers and magazines launched an all-out attack on Trump, slandering his name and reputation, mocking his agenda and depicting him as an outrageous spectacle — not a presidential candidate.

When Donald Trump won the presidential race in November 2016, the same media outlets that targeted him for negative reporting were left in shock. Their election predictions inaccurately portrayed a sure-win for Hillary Clinton. In fact, on November 8, 2016, *The New York Times* reported that Hillary Clinton had an 85% chance of winning.[2]

Trump's win caused Deep State influences within the media to reboot and launch an entirely new attack on the President's character, ability and policies. This was an attempt to not only take Trump down, but to give the illusion that his presidency was not the result of a fair election and the choice of the American people, but a scheme involving Russian interference that must be reversed.

In the first year of the Trump administration, media coverage of the incoming President was 90% negative.[3] In October of 2017, there were 41 positive statements about Trump in the media ... and 435 negative statements.[4]

On average, adults watch about 6.5 hours of news per week, much of this "news" from biased, left-leaning partisans and talking heads on stations like ABC, CNN and MSNBC.[5]

Mainstream media have devoted an enormous amount of coverage and airtime to the following topics, designed to systematically take down the President.

Over and over again, America sees, reads and hears about:

- Daily sensationalism in the Mueller investigation of President Trump's alleged collusion with Russia during the campaign. In reality, this investigation has exposed appalling Deep State bias within the intelligence agencies, Department of Justice and FBI (see Chapter Five), and hasn't produced a shred of evidence against Trump. In 2017, coverage of the Russia investigation accounted for one-fifth of all coverage of the President.[6]

- Highlights of angry, outraged protests against Trump's policies, such as the Women's Marches that called to "Impeach and Imprison" the President — giving the impression that the nation was outraged at Trump.

- Nonstop attention on Trump's wife, kids and his past. For example, alleged evidence of an extra-marital affair…years before Donald Trump was elected President.

- Over-the-top constant name-calling, including calling Trump "racist," "bigoted," and "mentally unstable."

- Speculations about Trump's personal finances and business dealings, completely unfounded and designed in a desperate attempt to discredit the President.

• And did I say, Russia, Russia, Russia?

Notice that the media spent almost all of its time discussing controversies and speculations — not policies and important domestic and international events. And, it's all an effort to distract and manipulate the public, presenting the perception of no positive reforms and policies.

Here's what the media did not cover, underplayed or slanted:

Trump's Historic Trip to the Middle East

The media paid little attention to Trump's historic trip to the Middle East, including Israel and Saudi Arabia, in May 2017. During this trip, the President:

• Met with leaders in one of the most conflict-ridden regions of the world

• Stood firm on foreign policy that pledged firm allegiance to Israel and to the destruction of Islamic terrorism.

• Met with a young Israeli girl, fulfilling her dream of meeting the President of the United States.

• Made a powerful speech in Saudi Arabia, where he spoke out against Islamic terrorist groups and the persecution of Christians and Jews, issues that are ignored by Islamic leaders and the media.

President Trump's "Promoting Free Speech and Religious Liberty"

"Promoting Free Speech and Religious Liberty" is

President Trump's Executive Order that helps protect the First Amendment rights of pastors.

Since 1954, the Johnson Amendment in the U.S. Tax Code has restricted pastors from speaking on political and cultural issues from the pulpit.

The media have neglected to cover this milestone in religious freedom. Instead, they have chosen either silence or mockery.

The Benefits of Trump's Tax Reform Plan

Deep State reporters, journalists and political pundits loved to speak out against President Trump's tax reform plan, saying it "destroy[s] the middle class" and only helps the rich.[7]

In reality, the tax reform plan:

- Puts more money back into the households of all Americans – up to a $4,000-per-family boost in income.[8]
- Protects tax benefits.
- Helps reduce crushing taxes and regulations on businesses.
- Creates millions of new jobs and powerfully boosts the economy.

Despite the outpour of negative reporting that backed up Deep State opposition, the media were proved wrong: President Trump has delivered tax relief, bonus checks and job growth.

A Skyrocketing Economy and Low Rates of Unemployment

Under President Trump, the economy has seen

incredible growth. But you'll rarely hear about that in Deep State-aligned media sources, which hate to admit or report about the President's success.

The proof, however, is clear.

In the first couple years of the Trump presidency:

- Economic growth boomed at 3% or above, creating jobs and new opportunities.[9]
- Unemployment rates hit a 17-year low.[10]
- Unemployment rates for blacks dropped to 5.9% — a record low since 1972.[11]
- Consumer confidence skyrocketed.

The media's response?

- Silent
- Negative
- Distorted

President Trump's Firm Stance Against Islamic Terrorism

The U.S. military has made massive advances against ISIS under Trump, with close to one-third of all territory in the Middle East (including key cities of Mosul and Raqqah) recaptured from the Islamic state in the first year of Trump's presidency.

ISIS is on the run. ISIS is facing constant defeats. ISIS is being made irrelevant by Trump.

And the media?

Deafening silence and a continual focus only on the negative.

The media rarely highlights President Trump's strong actions against Islamic terrorism, saving and protecting lives in the world's most conflicted and contentious region.

Unbelievably, neither has the slanted, Deep State-fueled media covered President Trump's specific economy-boosting measures, crackdown on terrorism of all kinds and unwavering defenses of religious freedom.

Instead, news commentators and journalists nitpick Trump's tweets, harp on his rambunctious and attention-grabbing personality and question his mental health. Some of the additional diversions of the media have included:

- Rachel Maddow of MSNBC, spending 20 minutes talking about Trump filing taxes with one conclusion — Trump filed taxes.

- CNN reporter Don Lemon refusing to cover Susan Rice's potentially illegal unmasking of names linked to Trump.

- Chris Cuomo of CNN, speculating about Trump's marriage, with all levels of outrageous claims and conspiracy theories.

- Endless false claims and lies about the fabricated Trump-Russia investigation, which has ultimately exposed horrific corruption in the Democratic Party and the U.S. Intelligence agencies (go to Chapter Five to read more).

Deep State influence within the media means that TV stations, social media, newspapers and news sites will use their influence to deliberately attack anyone who disagrees with their own agenda — even more so, anyone who wants to change the status quo – like Trump.

Remember, the Deep State doesn't care about upholding truth and integrity. They care about growing bigger, maintaining power and imposing their ideology on the rest of us.

#2 Biased Reporting of Current Events

"Reporting" is not objective. It is a biased, dangerous tool used by the Deep State to present a twisted reality to the American public. Their objective is growing, not downsizing, government. They want to protect the bureaucracy, not make it work for the people.

For example:

Mass Shooting and Violence: The Media's Chance to Push a Leftist Political and Ideological Agenda

In reporting on current events that include mass shootings, violence, demonstrations and marches, TV news stations will often glaze over facts and details that do not support their own viewpoint and narrative.

And, they will often take the opportunity to attack Conservatives and Christians.

Take the following examples...

- In November of 2017, a deranged shooter opened fire on a church in Texas, killing 26 people. One brave resident of the town, armed with a rifle, shot the shooter and prevented more deaths. But the media focused on gun control instead of focusing on the fact that a man with a gun helped stop the murderer and save more lives.

- In August of 2017, a group of white supremacists gathered to protest the removal of a statue of Confederate General Robert E. Lee in Charlottestville, Virginia. They first chanted hateful, white supremacist statements and then clashed with a band of Black Lives Matter activists and other counter-protestors. Then 20-year old white nationalist James Fields rammed his car into the peaceful counter-protesters, killing one person and injuring 19 others. That horrific day of hate was used by the media to smear true Conservatives, grouping them together with violent racists.

- In February of 2018, Nikolas Cruz, a former student at a high school in Parkland, Florida, opened fire on 17 students and faculty members. The resulting protests, supported by progressive groups and promoted by the media, involved thousands of high-school students who were used to support more gun control.

The Media Takes Aim at Trump's Foreign Policy

The media has mocked President Trump's pro-freedom, America-first foreign policy ever since he defeated Hillary Clinton in the 2016 presidential election.

Deep State-aligned TV and news stations criticized Trump's tough approach with North Korea — even after his summit meeting with Kim Jong-un, during which the leader of North Korea signed a document that stated that his country would work towards "complete denuclearization of the Korean peninsula." [12]

This agreement was historic, marking a significant shift in global safety and security, and yet Deep State media sources continued to mock President Trump after the meeting.

President Trump's withdrawal of the United States from the Paris Climate Accord was met with outrage from all over the world — even though his decisive action helped put millions of Americans back to work and spared taxpayers from funding this ridiculous, barely effective environmental policy.

And Trump's approach toward Iran has been severely attacked by the media since he announced that the United States has withdrawn from Obama's Iran nuclear deal.

Iran is the number-one state sponsor of terrorism in the world and should be dealt with accordingly. But *The New York Times* and *Newsweek* both scolded Trump over his statements about the Iranian government blocking social media sites.

"Trump bars Americans on Twitter but tells Iran to unblock social media sites," chimed *Newsweek* — as if the comparison was even remotely relevant.[13]

Deep State-fueled media sources portray current events with their own ideological spin — in an additional effort to promote their own agenda and manipulate the public.

#3 Internet Censorship

You may be surprised to learn that the Internet is not as "free" or open as you may think. The Deep State's left-wing bias and progressive agenda are everywhere on display on Facebook, Google, YouTube, Twitter and Amazon. They all manipulate and distort content and information that users are able to access.

As the largest open source of information in the world, the Internet has, in many ways, become an arm of the Deep State – a tool for censoring and silencing anyone who disagrees with its agenda.

Political bias and religious censorship and bigotry on Facebook

Facebook shows a nearly complete bias in support of a liberal, progressive ideology. In fact, it openly conducts business using a censorship of conservative, Christian values and opinions.

Take the following cases:

- A former Facebook employee admitted that Facebook manipulates its "trending" section by removing conservative political news — even though these posts and topics were popular among users.

- Facebook censors posts from many conservatives and Libertarians.

- Facebook has censored Christian bloggers for quoting the Bible and citing verses relating to homosexuality, marriage, abortion and other religious issues.

Facebook rules and regulations determine what is considered "hate speech" according to its own atheist, left-wing ideology — suppressing the voices of those who disagree with the views advanced by Facebook CEO Mark Zuckerberg.

Blacklisted from Google — Your Influence, Voice, and Presence Effectively Erased from the Internet

The world's biggest and most powerful search engine has strong, leftist political bias. It also has the power to manipulate search rankings, censor your search results, and blacklist anything with which its management disagrees.

During the 2016 presidential election, an algorithm used by Google ensured that "crooked" would not be automatically paired with "Hillary" when typed into the search field. However, when "lying" was typed in, it would automatically be paired with "Ted" (Cruz).

Google will blacklist individuals, accounts, and even businesses — for example, businesses that don't align with Google's social and political views are blacklisted from using AdWords, effectively destroying their chances of success when using the Internet.

Blacked Out on YouTube

In theory, YouTube is a great "equalizer" of content. Anyone can create his or her own channel and publish their own videos to reach a massive audience. Anyone can be heard, seen or even become famous.

However, censorship on YouTube is a real threat to those who might share conservative, libertarian or Christian content.

Popular radio host Dennis Prager has had dozens of videos blocked from public viewing by being put on a "restricted list."

The reason for the restriction? His videos portray content such as:

- "The Most Important Question About Abortion."
- "Where are the Moderate Muslims?"
- "Is Islam a Religion of Peace?"
- "The World's Most-Persecuted Minority: Christians."
- "Why America Must Lead."
- "The Ten Commandments: Do Not Murder."

Pro-life videos are also restricted on YouTube. One video exposing statistics about Planned Parenthood was immediately restricted, only hours after being released.

Singer Joyce Bartholomew's music video of her song celebrating a pro-life perspective was also removed... denying the right of musicians to express their political opinions through their music.

Videos you publish on YouTube will be free and accessible to the world...but only if their content reflects a Deep State-friendly ideology.

Killing Free Speech on Twitter

Twitter is a popular platform for sharing opinions and insights about culture, politics, religion and current events.

But a Deep State-backed "Trust and Safety Council" could limit the free speech of Conservatives, Libertarians and Christians if their tweets are interpreted as harassment. Who are the members of this "1984-like" "Safety Council"?

- Gay and Lesbian Alliance Against Defamation (which has turned into a virulent, hard-left interest group)

- Feminist Frequency (which monitors and attempts to censor free speech instead of actually promoting it)

- The Wahid Institute (an Indonesian Research Center dedicated to promoting "peaceful" Islam)

Given the list of members, it's pretty obvious who is going to be silenced — opponents of the Deep State.

Amazon Reviews — Erased and Forgotten if They Criticize Deep State Ideologues

Leaving a product review seems harmless enough … until that review doesn't agree with the Deep State ideology.

After Hillary Clinton published a book about being defeated by Donald Trump, Amazon deleted more than 900 negative reviews of the book.[14]

Amazon's far-left political bias extends even to

censoring honest opinions…so that even the credibility of books you might read and products you might use are distorted by their political agenda.

Collusion with the media is one of the most insidious and harmful tools used by the Deep State. By hiding the truth, distorting the facts, censoring free speech and allowing journalism to spiral into hate-mongering and sensationalism, the American media have betrayed the public — and proven to be a totally politicized tool of the Deep State.

CHAPTER 13

12 Examples of the Deep State's War on Christianity

Christians all over the world face the daily threat of violence, marginalization, discrimination, harassment, torture and death for their faith.

A new report from "Aid to the Church in Need" says that Christian persecution is actually worse today than ever before in recorded history.[1]

Violent terrorist groups like the Islamic State of Iraq and Syria (ISIS) in the Middle East and Boko Haram in Nigeria want to completely stamp out Christianity by using genocide and terror. Radical Hindus and Buddhists are actively trying to destroy Christianity in India and Myanmar. They see a belief in Christ as a threat to their power, and as incompatible with their own fundamentalist ideology of hatred and intolerance toward other religions.

In the United States, believers in Christ are not yet being subjected to widespread physical persecution for their faith.

Yet, over the last 20 years, a growing, systematic persecution of Christians has emerged in our culture and institutions. In fact, the worst persecution this nation has ever seen has all occurred during the last decade.

In our schools, in our workplaces, in courtrooms and in boardrooms, decisions are being made every day about what people should learn and believe...about how they should behave...and about what "religious freedom" actually means in our Constitutional Republic.

And its most aggressive attacks come from the anti-Christian hatred of the Deep State.

The result is a growing wave of intolerance, censorship and attempts to systematically marginalize, attack and exterminate Christian values from the fabric of American society.

Christians in the United States are being....

- robbed of their constitutionally guaranteed religious freedom to practice their faith in the public square, in their workplaces and in schools
- ostracized, mocked and persecuted for upholding and exercising their biblical values
- censored, attacked and silenced by mainstream media and on the Internet

Deep State ideology drives government bureaucrats, judicial activists and media elites to mock and suppress the right of Christians to religious freedom because it threatens the Deep State's ability to maintain power.

The U.S. Constitution expressly declares that we have the freedom to use free speech to express our beliefs and to practice our faith in public. In fact, it is the first right proclaimed in the Bill of Rights and the First Amendment to the United States Constitution; "Congress shall make no law respecting an establishment of religion or prohibiting the free exercise thereof, or abridging the freedom of speech..."

But despite the Constitution's ironclad guarantee of religious freedom, the Deep State wants to govern what you should believe and how you should practice your faith. And if your beliefs interfere with their own agenda, they will use funding, political manipulation and media to destroy you.

America's founders left their home countries in many cases because they were not allowed to practice their faith under the ruling systems of other nations. So at great risk, they left everything to practice religious freedom in a new nation.

But Deep State politicians and bureaucrats ignore the fact that the core foundations of the United States rest on Christian principles.

As our nation's Founders boldly proclaimed in the Declaration of Independence: "We hold these truths to be self-evident, that all men are created equal, that they are endowed by their Creator with certain unalienable Rights, that among these are Life, Liberty and the Pursuit of Happiness. That to secure these rights, Governments are instituted among Men, deriving their just powers from the consent of the governed."

Now, the very principles that this country were founded on are being attacked and suppressed by the Deep State. This ideological force doesn't want you to have the freedom to worship, evangelize, and live out the ideals of Scripture the way we are taught in the Bible.

The Deep State is waging war on Christianity.

Let's look specifically at government actions that have been an assault on people of religious faith:

Example 1: An Anti-Christian Ideological Agenda...Promoted Internationally by the U.S. State Department

The United States has historically helped advance Christian values among the nations of the world: freedom, justice and equality.

However, under the Obama administration, the State Department, which has long been a left-of-center organization, became even more radical and was transformed into a force for extreme progressive ideology and anti-Christian values.

And most of these political activists in the Obama State Department are still working in positions of authority and responsibility.

For example, instead of promoting religious freedom and human rights to nations in desperate need of freedom and reform, the State Department focused on advancing:

- The LGBT agenda
- Pro-abortion policies
- Socialism

But they remained silent on persecution worldwide of religious minorities — especially Christians.

The bottom line is that the State Department continues to be permeated by supporters of a radical ideology that undermines the foundations of religious freedom in the United States and for nations around the world.

Here are just a few examples of strategic and heartless choices that show a disturbing anti-Christian bias in the U.S. State Department:

- Obama issued a presidential memorandum that directed "all Federal agencies engaged abroad to ensure that U.S. diplomacy and foreign assistance *promote* (emphasis added) and protect the human rights of LGBT persons."[2]

- Obama holdovers have flown the gay pride flag at U.S. embassies all over the world in their rush to promote a pro-homosexual agenda abroad.

- The Obama administration also launched the "Global Equality Fund," a massive endowment spanning the public and private sector that poured $30 million into supporting an LGBT agenda in 80 different nations.[3]

- Obama supported funding for abortions overseas by rescinding the Mexico City Policy. Trump has reinstated the policy, with the potential to save millions of unborn lives by denying federal funding to organizations that perform abortions or provide propaganda supporting abortion.

- The Obama State Department also made massive grants through the United States Agency for International Development to George Soros' radical Open Society Foundations, which actively promotes unrest in countries with free market, pro-America values.

- The Obama State Department has ignored the horrific genocide of Christians in the Middle East, especially in Iraq and Syria, where radical Muslims are trying to systematically destroy Christians and exterminate them from these countries.

- The Obama State Department ignored persecuted Christians worldwide, allowing India, China, North Korea, Russia, Muslim countries and other states to impose harsh restrictions and persecution of evangelism, churches and Christianity.

- Under the Obama administration, the State Department fully supported the most anti-Israel, pro-Palestinian, pro-Muslim Brotherhood terrorist efforts in U.S. history.

The State Department, trumpeting its support of human rights, did little to actually do so because of its anti-Christian, anti-Western ideological positions.

Here's just one story of how the State Department ignored the appalling persecution of Christians overseas, and eventually capitulated under the pressure of outraged and deeply concerned U.S. citizens.

Mariam Ibrahim is a Sudanese woman who was going to be hanged because she refused to renounce her faith in Jesus Christ. She was condemned for apostasy and adultery in Sudan, and sentenced to hang. While in jail, she gave birth while still chained to the floor of the jail cell, then nursed her newborn along with taking care of her 2-year-old son. The State Department did nothing but issue toothless protests.

I started a petition to go nationwide, generating thousands of people to support, the release of Mariam. The Republicans and Conservatives in Congress were vocal advocates for the State Department to help free this woman. Nothing was done.

I finally went to Congresswoman Maxine Waters, told her about the plight of Mariam, and gave her the petitions signed by people in her district who wanted to have Mariam released. She was surprised at how many petition signers there were in her district. She had not even heard of the plight of this mother.

In response, Waters went to the Congressional Black Caucus and some of her other progressive friends with this injustice. Liberal Democrats signed a letter to John Kerry demanding that Mariam be released from prison. Three days later, she was released.

The State Department has tremendous authority and power. But there are Christian pastors and believers throughout the world who are American citizens and are being ignored by the State Department to this day.

The State Department has continued to resist change and undermine the Trump administration. Under

Deep State bureaucrats like Rex Tillerson's chief of staff Margaret Peterlin and senior policy advisor Brian Hook, resistance to President Trump's agenda only subsided when Secretary of State Mike Pompeo was sworn into office.

Peterlin and Hook worked tirelessly to take advantage of approximately 200 unfilled positions in the Department to advance their own agenda and keep Trump supporters out of U.S. embassies around the world. Experienced staffers and qualified candidates were often passed over for State Department jobs out of fear that they would promote Trump's "America First" approach to foreign policy.

Peterlin resigned after President Trump fired Rex Tillerson. But with more than 70,000 employees, there are still plenty of Deep State ideologues in the Department who are intensely opposed to Trump's conservative values. Using the authority, influence and power of the United States to promote progressive propaganda on the international stage, these government bureaucrats are damaging our relations with other nations by their socialist and progressive schemes and extreme anti-Christian bigotry.

Leaks, sabotage and refusal to do work continue.

Example #2: Using Obamacare to Try to Force Christians to Provide Contraceptives

The Constitution bars Congress from prohibiting the free exercise of religion or abridging the freedom of speech. But the Deep State has tried to impose its will on Christians, who believe that life begins at conception or that providing sexual contraceptives contradicts their religious beliefs.

Much of the bureaucracy — led by Deep State officials and operatives — has enforced policies that have denied freedom to Christians and forced them to violate their religious beliefs or be punished by government authorities.

The following disturbing examples should serve as a warning to us about how the Deep State demands that we conform to their value system without objection:

The Little Sisters of the Poor is a Catholic organization run by nuns that provides services to the elderly and other people in need. Obamacare tried to force the charity to provide services such as the so-called morning after or week-after pill (a drug that induces abortion) to their clients — despite this being a denial of their religious beliefs.

When the case was heard by the U.S. Supreme Court, the Little Sisters of the Poor won: A victory for religious freedom, but disturbing evidence of Deep State ideology attempting to control charitable and religious organizations.

Hobby Lobby also had its religious freedom case heard by the U.S. Supreme Court when it was forced to provide contraceptives to its employees under the Affordable Care Act. The owners of Hobby Lobby are strong Christians and are opposed to the use of contraceptives, but the ideologically driven system of Obamacare sought to force them into violating their religious beliefs.

Like the Little Sisters of the Poor, Hobby Lobby also won in court...but they had to fight hard against Deep State operatives who tried to enforce their ideologically driven rules and regulations at the expense of religious freedom.

The Deep State wants to interfere with the freedom

of individuals, nonprofits, businesses and other organizations by forcing them to participate in or support practices they deem immoral or that are in conflict with their deeply held religious beliefs.

Organizations such as the Little Sisters of the Poor and Hobby Lobby are winning in court – but it might only take a handful of judicial activists to reverse some of these important decisions and do great harm to religious freedom.

Example #3: Destroying Adoption

It seems reasonable that a Christian organization would choose to associate with people of the same faith.

But the LGBT lobby is attacking the right to exercise this religious freedom...specifically in the case of Christian adoption agencies, who pair foster children of all backgrounds and religions with families.

Miracle Hill is a Christian adoption agency in South Carolina that was told by the Department of Social Services that they cannot make religious beliefs a requirement of foster parents — effectively destroying their mission and robbing potentially thousands of parentless children of the opportunity to be adopted into loving homes.

Organizations similar to Miracle Hill have also been attacked — and forced to shut down their operations because they would not sacrifice their religious beliefs.

It's tragic...preventing thousands of orphaned children from being adopted by Christian parents who would embrace them with love and compassion.

Deep State ideologues don't care about the impact of their vicious legislation and restrictions on others, however. They care about legislating their principles into every business, organization and agency to the detriment of those with different beliefs.

Example #4: Silencing Christians on the News, Social Media, TV, and the Internet: Censorship of Christ in the Media

How often do you see Christian content on the news, on television, and on the internet?

Unless you're specifically looking for it, Christian opinions and information may be difficult to come by. In fact, many people in the United States don't even know about the Gospel of Jesus Christ because they have never read or heard about it.

That seems strange in a nation with roughly 230 million Christians…the largest Christian population in the world.[4,5]

It's no accident.

Censorship of Christians in the Media

The Deep State wants to suppress the spread of Christian principles and immutable values because it counteracts their own ideology. And they have partnered with the media to create an environment in which Christian thoughts and opinions are ignored or censored.

Major internet giants like Facebook, Amazon, Twitter and Google are run by people who want to advance a radical progressive agenda – so they will censor Christian-based information and opinions. They also have the ability to alter search results and algorithms to affect the kinds of information you receive on the

Internet.

Take a look at the following examples:

- Apple has taken down some Christian applications from its iTunes store, making them almost impossible to access or download. The reason? The Christian "apps" both express biblical views on marriage and homosexuality.

- YouTube has censored Catholic Online's videos with Scripture readings — despite the fact that these videos contain only content with Bible readings.

- Google for Nonprofits does not list churches and other religious organizations that apply biblical views on sexuality when hiring people. They also use algorithms in search results that intentionally exclude Christian viewpoints and organizations.

- Facebook censored an ad by Governor Mike Huckabee in support of Chick-Fil-A's stance on same-sex marriage.

- Twitter removed an ad by Tennessee Congresswoman Marsha Blackburn, who stands for biblical morality in her politics. The ad was deemed "inflammatory" because it opposed Planned Parenthood.

These are just a few of the countless examples of dangerous media censorship that has taken over our communication channels.

The Southern Poverty Law Center: Using Lies and Deceit to Manipulate Public Opinion

Much of the hatred directed at Christians in the media uses the Southern Poverty Law Center as a source. This organization, which has a preposterous "hate map" labeling Christian groups as hate groups, has been picked up by leftist news, like CNN and MSNBC.

Their "hate map" includes Alliance Defending Freedom — a conservative, Christian organization that defends religious freedom, and the Pacific Justice Institute — a conservative legal defense organization that provides civil liberties without charge.

They have also attacked such prominent and highly esteemed Christian leaders as Franklin Graham, son of the late Dr. Billy Graham and founder of Samaritan's Purse.

The SPLC's "hate map" was used by the U.S. military, Justice Department, and FBI until Donald Trump became President.

Persecution of Christianity in the media is real, influential, and it's dangerously shaping the perspective and opinions of a new generation.

Example #5: Christian Business Owners Attacked and Denied Their Rights to Believe in the Sanctity of Marriage

Christian business owners have also been strategically targeted and attacked by Deep State "judicial activists," who use lawsuits and other means in an attempt to deny them their First Amendment rights in order to advance the Deep State ideology.

Many of these cases involve business owners who refuse to compromise their values on family and marriage — and who are then accused of racism, bigotry and illegal discrimination, and any other smear that they can concoct.

Masterpiece Bakery. Jack Phillips is a Colorado-based baker who was approached by a homosexual couple asking him to bake a wedding cake for their ceremony. When Phillips told them he could not bake a cake for them with a pro-gay message because of his religious beliefs, the couple sued him. Phillips argued that baking a cake for two men with a pro-homosexual message is a creative expression that would go against his belief system; but Colorado argued otherwise. Phillips won in the U.S. Supreme Court.

Tastries Bakery. In a similar case, bakery owner Cathy Miller was also sued by the state of California for declining to bake a wedding cake for a same-sex couple. Miller won in court on the grounds that baking a cake is artistic expression, and therefore an expression of free speech.

Barronelle Stutzman. Stuzman is a florist who was fined for refusing to provide her services for a same-sex wedding on the grounds that she was exercising her constitutional rights as set forth in the First Amendment. Stutzman eventually lost in court.

Hands On Originals. Blaine Adamson owns a custom Christian apparel shop in Kentucky. Adamson was taken to court for refusing to make T-shirts for a gay pride festival. He won his case in the Kentucky Court of Appeals.

Elane Photography. Elaine Huguenin of Elane Photography was taken to the New Mexico Supreme Court for refusing to photograph a same-sex commitment ceremony. Huguenin made the argument that she could not use artistic expression to communicate a message at odds with her Christian beliefs.

Elane Photography lost in the New Mexico Supreme Court. In one shocking expression of totalitarian, anti-Christian bigotry, Justice Richard Bosson wrote that Elaine and her husband, Jonathan, were now "compelled by law to compromise the very religious beliefs that inspire their lives" as "it is the price of citizenship."[6]

What these judicial radicals would really like is for Christians to disobey their core beliefs in order to become compliant, nonresisting "citizens" of a Deep State-run nation.

Atlanta Fire Chief Kelvin Cochran. Atlanta Fire Chief Kelvin Cochran lost his job after self-publishing a book about manhood from a biblical perspective. Cochran led the fire department to a Class 1 rating for the first time, had saved numerous lives and risen from poverty. But his book — which made brief mention of biblical sexuality — caused leftist outrage. Cochran lost his job after the Mayor of Atlanta spoke out openly against the contents of Cochran's book.

Example #6: Not Even Our Children Are Safe — Deep State Social Engineering in Our Public Schools

An entire generation is being indoctrinated with dangerous, liberal ideology that mocks Christianity and suppresses the truth.

In public schools all over the nation, the Deep State is working through the Department of Education, state governments, local school districts, and teachers to promote:

- The LGBT agenda, promoting an ideology of homosexuality and transgenderism
- Vicious attacks against homeschooling, in an attempt to destroy parental rights and Christian education

- Discrimination against prayer in schools, barring students from openly praying on campus

The LGBT agenda, encouraged and promoted ... to children as young as 3 or 4

Children as young as 3 or 4 years of age are being taught in government-run schools the lie that gender is a choice – and if they're confused about their sexuality, they can switch from girl to boy or boy to girl.

In fact, young children are having sex-change operations — and being given the right to "decide their gender" when they are barely past the age of infancy.

This shocking curriculum is even being rewritten to assert that certain historical figures were gay or transgender.

In California, elementary-school students learn about homosexuals and transgender people in history, comparing them to minority groups who have fought for their civil rights — such as blacks.

And outside of the classroom, young children are given the choice to use transgender bathrooms, or they must go to the bathroom with children of the opposite sex.

Prayer, the Bible and the Gospel in schools: suppressed and shut down

The right of a child to pray or read the Bible in school is being attacked, and in many cases is being forbidden despite rulings by the U.S. Supreme Court allowing such. Judges, school districts and nonprofits have colluded with Deep State bureaucrats to attack and punish kids who want to express their religious beliefs.

In Tennessee, one Bible club for first- and second-graders was attacked and shut down because it was deemed "unconstitutional" by the Freedom From Religion Foundation — a Deep State nonprofit that ironically robs people of their religious freedom.

In other cases, young students have been suspended for sharing their beliefs with other students. Michael Leel is a high school student who was suspended three times for sharing his Christian faith on campus. He was forced to leave, miss class and possibly fall behind in his studies because he wanted to tell his friends and peers about God.

Bureaucrats, school officials, judicial activists and politicians who are aligned with Deep State ideology are actively influencing public education in America. They know that if they can begin manipulating children at an early age, they will produce more radicals like them: people driven by leftist ideology and devoted to power and control.

Example #7: Explosion of Transgender Ideology

A tiny fraction of the United States population self-identifies as "transgender," estimated at 0.58%.[7] A large percentage of this extremely small number of individuals includes teenagers who have been brainwashed into questioning their own gender.

The explosion of transgender ideology in schools, public facilities, and even nursing homes might cause you to believe that the actual number is higher.

Public schools aren't the only place where the idea of transgenderism is pushed on vulnerable or disturbed people.

In California, a law has made it possible for nursing

home residents to use the bathroom of their gender "identity" rather than their biology. The law also heavily penalizes nursing home workers for using the "wrong" pronoun when referring to residents who consider themselves "transgender."

Obama's removal of the ban on transgenders serving in the military also marked a radical shift — affecting a tiny population of transgender people who want to join the military (and have the taxpayers pay for their sex-change operation). It caused delays, distraction and chaos in the arm of the government that plays a vital role in our protection and security.

Trump reinstated the ban, but the Deep State backlash was immediate, outrageous and furious.

It's more evidence that in their workplaces, schools, and in public areas, Christians are forced to participate and comply with a dangerous ideology that goes against their religious beliefs. Their right to practice their faith has been snuffed out, in the name of "tolerance."

Example #8: The Deep State's Pro-abortion Assault on Life

Abortion is a central pillar of Deep State ideology. They want to suppress and silence the belief that human life begins at conception — and compel hard-working Christians and like-minded pro-life Americans to fund abortion with their tax dollars.

Every year, the federal government gives Planned Parenthood more than $500 million in funding — taken out of taxpayer dollars.[8] Planned Parenthood uses the funds for a variety of services — abortion being the reason for the group's existence. In fact, Planned Parenthood performs hundreds of thousands of abortions every year – 321,384 abortions in 2016 ... and reportedly sells fetal tissue.[9]

When this despicable funding is challenged, Deep State bureaucrats are outraged.

The Deep State won't stop at funding pro-abortion clinics, which are basically killing factories designed to exterminate unborn babies. They want to expand their control to pro-life clinics, which offer women with unplanned pregnancies adoption services and other alternatives to abortion.

In California, Governor Jerry Brown signed a bill that forced pro-life clinics to advertise free or low-cost abortions in their waiting rooms — promoting the very crime against humanity that they are fighting to eradicate. The law has been ruled unconstitutional in state courts and the case has been taken to the Supreme Court.

This is the Deep State at work ... to impose progressive ideology on anyone who values life ... and spread the idea that the murder of a baby is simply the removal of "fetal tissue."

The Bible says,

"Before I formed you in the womb, I knew you.."

(Jeremiah 1:5)

"For you created my inmost being; you knit me together in my mother's womb ... My frame was not hidden from you when I was made in the secret place, when I was woven together in the depths of the earth. Your eyes saw my unformed body; all the days ordained for me were written in your book before one of them came to be."

(Psalm 139: 13, 15-16)

Yes, an unborn life is still a human life!

A Deep State, pro-abortion agenda must silence the voices of those who oppose the mass murder of unborn babies.

Example #9: Pastors, Silenced From the Pulpit

For 60 years, the government has threatened to punish houses of worship and their leaders if they say something that is deemed "too political."

This imposition and violation of free speech is enforced by the Johnson amendment, which puts Christian pastors and other clergy or 501(c)(3) at risk of losing their tax exemption status for speaking out against the policies or actions of elected officials and candidates.

The Deep State has defended the continuation of this unfair law because it silences voices of faith from commenting on important moral and social issues... knowing that pastors, priests, rabbis and other religious leaders will, in many cases, endorse candidates who do not comply with their own radically progressive ideology.

The First Amendment guarantees the right of religious leaders to speak on cultural and political issues...on whatever is relevant and important to their congregants.

President Trump has made important progress in reclaiming our First Amendment Right to the free exercise of religious faith, with his Executive Order "Promoting Free Speech and Religious Liberty."

That order, signed on last year's National Day of Prayer, dictates that the IRS use "maximum enforcement discretion" on all matters relating to the Johnson

Amendment.

The Deep State is fighting hard to silence Christianity in America.

Deep State operatives in the U.S. State Department are advancing a deceptive, anti-Christian "Voice of America" all over the world.

Christians are denied their freedom to act according to their consciences and religious beliefs.

Judicial radicals and statists are suppressing our individual rights to religious freedom — especially when it comes to followers of Jesus Christ.

Censorship in the media is producing a warped, false view of Christians and Christianity – and silencing anyone who dares to express their faith.

Deep State bureaucrats are working furiously and every day to write into law rules and regulations that persecute and penalize Christians for their beliefs.

Deep State agents and their clueless pawns in America's public education system are attempting to indoctrinate the next generation with their own ideology...and punish children who practice their faith in school.

And the federal government is funding the murder of hundreds of thousands of unborn children every year — with your hard-earned tax dollars.

The Deep State targets the Trump administration again and again — but President Donald Trump has stood up for America's Christians and their First Amendment rights.

The U.S. Department of Health and Human Services has redefined life as beginning at conception, a great milestone for the pro-life fight against the murders of the innocent.

President Trump has also cut U.S. funding to the United Nations Population Fund, because it participates in China's forced-abortion policies, and reinstated the Mexico City policy, which denies aid money from the United States going to any international non-governmental organization (NGO) that promotes or funds abortion.

President Trump has also nominated strict constructionists to the federal judiciary and U.S. Supreme Court — not judicial activists – judges who will not legislate their ideology from the bench, but who will uphold the Constitution — and the rights of Christians.

CHAPTER 14

The False Hope: Eight Reasons the Deep State Bureaucracy Cannot Be Fixed

You need to be aware that there is a false hope that the Deep State bureaucracy can be fixed, reformed and made efficient.

Many believe a few fringe bureaucrats are to blame for the corruption and inefficiency of our government agencies. Simply fire the "bad players" and hire more honest people and better managers. This way, we can control and correct the Deep State abuse of power.

Can the Deep State bad players be reformed?

Can "cleaning house" solve the problem?

Can hiring more honest and efficient people do the trick?

Let's see if this is possible:

Deep State corruption of power and political bias have infiltrated the top levels of management of the entire federal government bureaucracy. This is not an isolated problem.

Just as disturbing is the fact that lower levels of bureaucracy are infected with just as much bias.

The reality is that at all levels of bureaucracy, government employees secretly and illegally use the power of the state to:

- Stop change
- Evade detection and transparency
- Promote a political ideology

You see that the bureaucracy itself is corrupt. The bureaucratic culture has been infected from the top down.

The growth of the bureaucracy is one of the most dangerous realities of the Deep State:

- It endangers our freedom.
- It endangers our economic growth.
- It endangers our future.

As you learned about in Chapter Four, the bureaucracy is built on an ideology of big government control and wasteful spending. It overregulates, stifles entrepreneurship and innovation. The bureaucracy lives to grow itself, justify its own existence and trample individual freedom and constitutional rights.

The truth is, a few "bad" bureaucrats aren't responsible for the appalling waste and inefficiency of government agencies. "Good" bureaucrats won't fix it. The bureaucracy is inherently destructive.

It's the nature of the bureaucracy that continues to threaten individual liberty and our Democratic Republic.

It's the nature of bureaucracy that it can't be fixed by more regulations, taxes or laws ... or more honest politicians.

Here are eight little-known ways that the bureaucracy has allowed and encouraged Deep State abuses of power – and why the bureaucracy will always fail, even at the local and state levels.

1. Throughout history, bureaucracies have always abused their power.

The bigger the bureaucracy, the greater the loss of

individual freedom and human rights.

History is filled with government abuses of power. For example, well-known abuses of power in recent history include those in Nazi Germany, Soviet Russia and Communist China. These are all examples of bureaucracies under socialist governments that have been destructive to people, progress and freedom.

Bureaucracies will always abuse their power, because it's human nature to do so.

It's the nature of individuals to act in their own self-interest.

In the private sector, as 18th-century economist and philosopher Adam Smith pointed out, man's self-interest will ultimately benefit the consumer.

But that's not the case with government. In the government, the power of bureaucracy results in the worst of human nature – demanding power and control without regard for others. Acting in their own collective self-interest and in the interests of the bureaucracy itself, bureaucrats will use the power of the state to protect their control, achieve their goals and promote serfdom.

The Founding Fathers of the United States set up a system to ensure that this harmful aspect of human nature remains in check.

But the Deep State has grown out of control, and our constitutional rights are ignored

- Bureaucrats want conformity.
- Bureaucrats want compliance.
- Bureaucrats want power.

Combine these three motives with little accountability or transparency, and you have a perfect environment for abuse of power.

Then combine the above with an ideology that wants to transform our culture and economy — an ideology of superiority that must use the power of the state to implement policy and change – and abuse of power is the outcome.

Today, the Deep State abuses its power with its war on Trump ... its war on capitalism ... its war on Christianity ... its war on freedom. And finally, it's being exposed. But this exposure will not end the dangerous abuses of power.

Bureaucracts can and will arrogantly expand their power. This tendency is inherent to the bureaucracy, and it's inherent to government.

A free country will have a small bureaucracy, limited in power and reach. A free people is not bullied by unelected bureaucrats demanding obedience and controlling all aspects of public and private life.

2. Bureaucrats are not usually accountable to punishment.

If a private company tries to exploit a customer, vendor or even competitor, the fear of a lawsuit prevents or stops the abuse.

But a government bureaucrat or agency who mistreats the public or private business, fails to perform or makes a mistake:

- Is unlikely to ever be discovered
- Faces little or no opposition
- Is unlikely to be punished even if exposed

Frédéric Bastiat was a brilliant French writer and economist in the 1840's who knew that bureaucratic government control over the individual would result in an abuse of power. He advocated against empowering the French to create bureaucracies in his brilliant book *The Law*, still powerful and relevant today.

Bastiat said, "All these vital forces of society should develop harmoniously under the influence of liberty and that none of them should become, as we see has happened today, a source of trouble, abuses, tyranny, and disorder."[1]

The misdeeds of the bureaucracy – ineffectiveness, destructive decisions or worse – are always hidden or covered up.

The FBI/Department of Justice scandal is a great example of a cover-up in the bureaucracy.

At first, government employees in the intelligence agencies thought they would never be caught. Then they tried to hide their abuse. They resorted to lying and distorting facts. They said they lost or couldn't find emails, text messages or other documents. They refused to respond to congressional demands for documentation.

Their arrogance reflected a sense of moral righteousness, and a belief that the bureaucracy had to be protected at all costs and that the ends justified the means.

But this scandal isn't the first time that corruption has been found in the FBI. For years, it has acted as a rogue agency conducting illegal and unethical prosecutions using entrapment, threats, financial ruin and character assassination — all for the agency to win a conviction, often based upon a bureaucrat wanting to get ahead or to advance an ideological viewpoint.

The Departments of Interior, Education, Defense and other federal agencies rarely, if ever, have their policies and bureaucratic decisions challenged, exposed or punished for abuse. Yet abuse is happening, because that's the nature of bureaucracy.

3. Bureaucrats are unable to measure their success – and remain inefficient and unproductive.

In private business, we measure success in a variety of ways, including profits, sales, production, cost saving and much more. As a small business owner, I have had to measure all activity in an accountable way to survive and to profit.

Free markets compel us to measure success, which benefits the consumer, creates more jobs, generates higher paying jobs, motivates technological expansion and stimulates innovation and growth.

But government bureaucracy has little or no ability to measure success.

The goal of the bureaucracy is not to create a profitable, beneficial model of growth or organizational outcomes. Its goal is to:

- Hide problems from superiors
- Hide problems from heads of agencies
- Hide problems from Congress

Bureaucrats are not accountable for success, efficiency or cutting waste.

Instead, the bureaucracy creates a monster, eating tax dollars without measurable results or accountability.

That's why we see agencies that spend millions on ineffective programs and pay bloated salaries to their employees … and yet, are never shut down or reduced in size.

The needless duplication of jobs in the University of

California (UC) system is just one example of how the bureaucracy is responsible for appalling waste. At UC San Diego, the university pays dozens of employees in each division salaries of over $100,000 – all to do the same thing. Take a look at the following list of departments and positions at this bloated school bureaucracy, all responsible for the same task of "diversity."

- Chancellor's Diversity Office
- Vice Chancellor for Equity, Diversity, and Inclusion
- Assoc. Vice Chancellor for Faculty Equity
- Asst. Vice Chancellor for Diversity
- Faculty Equity Advisors
- Graduate Diversity Coordinators
- Staff Diversity Liaison
- Undergrad Student Diversity Liaison
- Graduate Student Diversity Liaison
- Director of Development for Diversity Initiatives
- Chief Diversity Officer
- Office of Academic Diversity and Equal Opportunity
- Committee on Gender Identity and Sexual Orientation Issues
- Campus Council on Climate, Culture, and Inclusion
- Diversity Council
- Cross-Cultural Center Director
- Lesbian, Gay, Bisexual, Transgender Resource Center Director

While students pay higher tuitions for schools, school bureaucracies continue to grow themselves with excessive salaries, unnecessary employees and duplication.

4. The bureaucracy ignores the harmful costs of its rules, regulations and programs.

If a private company makes a harmful decision, it will be quickly discovered and corrected.

But not a bureaucratic decision — the damages and abuses of the bureaucracy may be hidden and unaccountable, but they are real.

In Frédéric Bastiat's essay, "What is Seen and What is Not Seen," he rightly pointed out how government will focus on perceived benefits of an institution, regulation or law, but ignore the costs and often unintended consequences.

Bastiat gave two powerful examples:

- If you cut the military, there would be a loss of jobs. However, this loss ignores the fact that new jobs would also be created, as taxpayers were able to keep more of their income and spend it on consumer goods and new businesses.

- Special trade regulations in the iron industry would save mining jobs. However, the unseen consequences of this restriction would include the loss of other jobs that would be created by imported iron – including metal workers, nail workers and blacksmiths.

Today, the bureaucracy imposes excessive restrictions and regulations on our economy, preventing growth, job and income creation, innovations and other benefits. These are the unintended consequences of their programs, mandates and regulations.

For example, the unintended consequence of the United States Postal Service has been to create a harmful monopoly on mail delivery, as you discovered in Chapter Three. By eliminating this monopoly, competition would be stimulated and consumers would receive superior options for mail delivery.

Here are a few additional examples of how bureaucratic programs and subsidies have had a devastating impact on society – even though the intentions may have been good.

- **Traditional welfare** – enables people to work less, be less productive and even form single-parent families to earn greater benefits.

- **Ethanol subsidies** – increase food prices by using a significant amount of the U.S. corn crop, and reduce the availability of cropland for other types of food.

- **Business subsidies** – reduce incentives for companies to innovate new technologies, products and services to make a greater profit.

- **Disability benefits** – encourage people who are able to work to drop out of the labor force, damaging the economy.

- **Government programs for the poor and disenfranchised** – reduce the need for private charity, which is more effective and efficient at helping those who really need it.

5. Bureaucrats have no profit/loss incentive for excellence.

In a private business, you are forced to be efficient. As a small business owner, I have had to cut waste, hire only the best and spend carefully and wisely.

I'm forced to be efficient, or I go out of business.

In fact, I profit by being excellent and I'm harmed if I'm not.

But government doesn't operate that way.

Go to the Department of Motor Vehicles. Are you the priority? No. You are a nuisance. Did they ask how you are today? Probably not. Most likely DMV employees seemed overwhelmed and perhaps even complained about too much work, too much pressure and too many people.

Customer service is not held to a standard of excellence in government bureaucracy, because they are not motivated by measuring profit/loss. So, the outcome is agencies that run poorly and inefficiently.

Mediocrity and poor service are common to bureaucracies, because they don't have a profit/loss incentive.

6. Bureaucrats have no incentive to reduce or control costs and stop waste.

In a private company, you must keep costs low. You get competitive bids.

You make sure there is no waste.

But a bureaucracy has no incentive to lower costs — instead, they consistently demand more money to solve their perceived problems.

Take a look at education: We are finding that private schools, home schools, Christian schools and even charter schools that have the freedom to operate like a private school are flourishing. Kids are succeeding, teachers are innovating and the schools are booming with success.

What about public schools? They keep failing. Children aren't adequately educated. Tax payers must pay more and more. And parents do not see the outcomes they want from their children's education.

The bureaucracy says the solution is more money.

Bonds are passed. More tax revenues are allocated. The bureaucracy grows. Bureaucrats receive higher incomes. Departments hire more employees.

The schools? They get little or nothing. The students? They get little or nothing. The teachers? They get little or nothing. The failure continues. And the solution? More money, more money, more money.

Without incentives to reduce and control costs and waste, school bureaucracies have become giant cesspools of expense, waste and inefficiency.

7. Bureaucracies never die.

President Ronald Reagan once said, "a government bureau is the nearest thing to eternal life we'll ever see on this earth."[2]

And it's true.

A private company will go bankrupt if it continues with ineffective business activities that the marketplace doesn't want. But a bureaucracy can continue in operation by providing marginal or unneeded services.

In a private business, you're constantly looking at the bottom line for efficiency based upon what the marketplace says.

In a government setting, there is no accountability for poor outcomes. If there's a downturn in productivity, no one knows. If there is reduced quality, no one knows. But the taxpayer and public are hurt.

In private business, new technology and changes in the market eliminate products and services that are no longer needed.

I started my marketing and advertising agency out of college. In five years, I had 30 employees. Seven of them were typists, who had to spend hours typing documents multiple times.

As soon as technology improved, we ended this practice out of a need to stay efficient and competitive.

This is not the case with government. In California, there are more than 1,000 boards and agencies that are totally unnecessary in operation. In fact, these boards and agencies effectively produce nothing of value for society. They only add bloated salaries to the politically appointed czars and their armies of bureaucrats.

Auditors and politicians have decried these useless boards and agencies as wastes of taxpayer money. But nothing is ever done to remedy the problem.

Unnecessary or terribly performing government agencies don't downsize, transform or go bankrupt. They become permanent fixtures.

Free enterprise produces the greatest allocation of resources. But government/socialist policies are stuck in obsolete activities that become politicized if anyone suggests changing their infrastructure or shutting them down.

8. Central planning never has and never will work – because of bureaucracy.

The free market implicitly considers the billions of decisions being made by consumers every day and determines how much a product or service is needed, when it's needed and where it's needed. No bureaucrat can ever do this.

F.A. Hayek said in the book *The Road to Serfdom*, "It is the very complexity of the division of labor under modern conditions which makes competition the only method by which such coordination can be adequately brought about."[3]

And in *Capitalism and Freedom*, Dr. Milton Friedman argued that "The characteristic feature of action through political channels is that it tends to require or enforce substantial conformity. The great advantage of the market, on the other hand, is that it permits wide diversity."[4]

Central planning will only produce a stifled economy where citizens suffer from needless rules and regulations coming from bureaucrats who remain unaccountable for their actions.

A Socialist "Utopia" : The Final Outcome of Bureaucracy

Bureaucracy is core to a socialist belief system, as you'll discover in the following chapter.

Bureaucrats have no way to properly allocate resources or ensure efficiency. Bureaucrats act as an island to themselves. They act on their own will, do what they can to survive and expand their power, and aren't subject to any consequences.

When I was in college, I had the privilege of being invited to a lecture with Dr. Ludwig von Mises, a famous economist. In that meeting, I was introduced to a man who understood the inevitable failure of bureaucracy. And in fact, he wrote a book about bureaucracy.

Mises summed it up very well. He said, "The champions of socialism call themselves progressives, but they recommend a system which is characterized by rigid observance of routine and by a resistance to every kind of improvement.

"They call themselves liberals, but they are intent upon abolishing liberty.

"They call themselves democrats, but they yearn for dictatorship.

"They call themselves revolutionaries, but they want to make the government omnipotent.

"They promise the blessings of the Garden of Eden, but they plan to transform the world into a gigantic post office. Every man but one a subordinate clerk in a bureau."

Mises saw that bureaucracies are self-interested and economically irrational. He knew that there would be no reinventing of government so that bureaucracy could work better. By its nature, bureaucracy would lead to failure, corruption and abuse of power. By its nature, it would lead to the Deep State.

History shows us that the bigger the government is, the less the freedom, choice and prosperity of the individual.

Our nation was set up as a limited government with checks and balances. But as the government has gotten bigger, the individual has become smaller.

And, as the bureaucracy grows, the power of the individual shrinks.

The bureaucracy leads to economic distress, moral failure and abuse of power. It leads to the nefarious creation of the Deep State.

It's time to downsize government.

It's time to make the government smaller.

It's time to restore the American dream.

CHAPTER 15
The Deep State: The Road to Socialism

The most passionate defenders of the Deep State are socialists.

Socialists believe that bureaucracy is good and necessary. But this fundamental belief is where the socialists are dead wrong. The bloated bureaucracy is neither good, nor necessary, as you read about in Chapter Four and Chapter Fourteen.

Socialists believe in big government. But the history of big government is a history of failure.

Socialism always fails ... and always results in oppression, corruption and abuse of power.

And yet, there have been powerful leaders in the U.S. government who are socialists — for example, former Director of National Intelligence James Clapper and former CIA director John Brennan, whom you read about in Chapter Five.

A socialist, Deep State agenda continues to infiltrate more than just the intelligence agencies ... or the federal government.

Socialism has penetrated the government at the state and local levels, the judiciary, the media, the non-profit sector and more.

A socialist agenda attempts to suppress freedom and destroy the foundations of our nation in both the public and private sector ... so that the voice of its opposition is silenced.

In the following pages, you'll discover why socialism will always fail ... why socialism will hurt you and your family … and what you can do to help stop the rise of this dangerous belief system.

A Disturbing Affinity for Socialism is on the Rise

Winston Churchill famously called socialism "the philosophy of failure" saying that its "inherent virtue is the equal sharing of misery."[1]

Churchill knew that the "inherent virtue" of socialism is that it prevents economic growth and productivity.

But according to a recent survey by the American Culture & Faith Institute, four out of 10 Americans today prefer socialism to capitalism.[2]

Forty percent is a significant minority – and most likely includes Deep State sympathizers that are pushing for a radically progressive economic and social agenda in America.

Deep State sympathizers like Senator Bernie Sanders, Governor Jerry Brown and Senator Elizabeth Warren advocate different forms of socialism. Their brand of socialism promotes an increase in government bureaucracy, federal programs and strict regulations.

However, many people may not be aware that socialism does more than generate extra regulations and enlarge the bureaucracy.

Socialism, by its very nature, creates poverty, stagnation and oppression.

In reality, socialism will do nothing but harm Americans – including you and your family. Here are 10 reasons why:

1. Socialism creates a strong — and unresponsive — federal government.

The federal government has been assigned a

limited role which focuses on national defense and enforcement of the law. The Constitution promotes a system of checks and balances and separation of powers to ensure that the government does not overstep its boundaries.

However, socialism is contrary to the values and foundations of our nation. It creates a large, ineffective federal government that does not serve the people well.

2. Socialism creates an inefficient and ineffective bureaucracy. Bureaucracies are unaccountable entities that constantly want to grow and expand, but are always inefficient and ineffective. You've read about many of these government agencies in Chapter Three. Here's a quick re-cap:

- The United States Post Office: The U.S. Postal Service faces a crushing $65 billion bailout and benefit liability, with ongoing discussions about reducing days of service to five — even three days.

- Veterans Administration Hospitals: Patients have died on secret waiting lists. Administrators have not only not been held accountable for this, but have even gotten raises and promotions while people do not receive the care they need on their watch.

- The Department of Education: States are required to comply with overbearing mandates and regulations in order to receive federal funding, creating more red tape and challenges to educating the next generation.

3. Socialism crushes economic growth. Economic growth means new jobs are created, incomes go up and entrepreneurial opportunities boom. But socialism destroys economic growth. Socialism creates redistribution of wealth rather than creating more jobs and higher profits.

Socialists think of the economy as a pie, and central planners have to divide up what already exists. In a free economy, the pie grows larger so that even the poorest become richer.

4. Socialism kills innovation and progress. Socialism discourages individuals from creating new technologies, products or services. Government bureaucracies don't reward risk; they stifle innovation.

5. Socialism discourages entrepreneurship. While capitalism gives people equal opportunities to thrive and prosper, socialism simply ensures equal results. That means people are robbed of their motivation to start new businesses and discouraged by red tape and regulations.

6. Socialism wastes resources and money. In a capitalist society, there are harsher penalties for a business that fails, because it will run out of resources. But in a socialist society, the government may allocate an incredible amount of resources to a bureaucracy that is performing poorly, meaning money, time and resources are wasted.

As economist Milton Friedman said, "Nobody spends somebody else's money as carefully as he spends his own. Nobody uses somebody else's resources as carefully as he uses his own."[3]

7. Socialism relies on a federal top-down approach that can't match the free market. A free economy is self-correcting because it acts out of self-interest, not a top-down approach. For example, stimulus dollars just create billions of dollars of waste, a massive government failure.

8. Socialism means everyone is equally poor, except for an elite few. Socialism can degenerate into political corruption, causing the ruling elite to become extremely wealthy while the rest of the country suffers. People may be struggling to put dinner on the table in a suffering economy, while the government freely hands out benefits and resources to the politically connected.

Take the example of Venezuela: 87% of people who live in this "socialist utopia" say they don't have enough money to buy food.[4] A country with the largest oil reserves in the world should be extremely prosperous, but because the corrupt government controls the oil industry, the vast majority of Venezuelans cannot benefit from the existence of this rich resource.

The government does, however, make sure an elite few are well-off.

In fact, today, Hugo Chavez's daughter is the richest woman in the country, with $4.2 billion – although her own father once declared that the rich are "lazy."[5] In a country like Venezuela – which used to be the richest country in Latin America – socialism has induced tragic poverty and extreme political corruption.

9. Socialism encourages centralized power. Socialism has a history of failure: Nazism (National Socialism) in Germany; Fascism in Italy; Communism in Russia.

The genius of the United States Constitution prevents the creation of centralized power that will result in coercion and dictatorship. Nowhere in recorded history does democratic socialism not lead to political and economic distortions and oppression.

Consider Venezuela, as discussed above, where socialist policies have led to rationing of food and water, rationing of toiletries and other basic necessities, devaluation of the nation's currency, massive closures of small businesses and the flight of investment and capital out of the country.

Socialism has only led to tyranny, corruption and failure throughout the world, throughout history.

10. Socialism works against human nature. People will work harder to support themselves and their families than they will to make money for the government. Likewise, they will also take care of their own resources more carefully than they will take care of someone else's.

This was the early lesson of the Pilgrims, who came to America to escape persecution from the English government. In order to fund their new colony, they arranged a contract with companies called "adventures" that would provide them what they needed, evenly divided among all colonists. At the end of seven years, all profits from their colony's enterprise would be evenly divided among the Pilgrims and adventurers.

The problem was this: Everyone was required to work for everyone else, and given the same amount of food, regardless of individual need. The system bred deep resentment among the new colonists.

After the colony grew sicker, weaker and hungrier after more than two years of work, the Pilgrims abandoned their socialist experiment. They established a new system in which every family was responsible for itself and became extremely industrious. They planted more crops and eventually reaped a great harvest.

Given the lesson learned four centuries ago by those who founded this nation, it should be obvious that the socialist experiment does not result in prosperity. But the Deep State still advocates socialist tenets.

They ignore the intellectual, economic and moral bankruptcy of socialism, and instead want to find all their solutions in the federal government.

In fact, their god has become the government. It becomes the perfect answer for any problem. The state is worshiped. The individual is sacrificed to the collective.

And as a result, individual freedom, liberty of conscience and human choice are sacrificed and crushed for the benefit of the state.

A Final Word

Socialism cannot and will not help create an America that is prosperous and free.

A socialist agenda — central to Deep State ideology — is working to impede economic growth, waste our taxpayer dollars, corrupt our government agencies, and destroy conservative and Christian values.

We Must Fight the Deep State!

The Deep State is the result of a government that's too big, too powerful and too unaccountable.

It's the poisonous fruit and curse of a misguided belief in government control, bureaucracy and socialism.

But the record of history is clear: Socialism destroys individual freedom, produces failure and crushes economic growth, innovation and productivity. It rules through coercion. The Deep State bureaucracy of today is so big, so inefficient and so thirsty for power that it exists only to serve itself – and not the people.

Progressive and socialists will do or demand whatever it takes to protect and grow the bureaucracy — and make government ever stronger and more powerful — even though that means robbing you of your rights.

It's time to fight back, reclaim our constitutional rights, and stand up for what is right, true and just.

We must fight for individual freedom and oppose socialism — or whatever name it uses to deceive and enslave — progressive, Marxist or communist. We must fight for liberty, for free enterprise and for our God-given right to worship, speak and live in an America free from government tyranny and oppression.

Here is what must be done:

1. We must restore integrity, honesty, and trust in the Department of Justice, FBI and our national security and intelligence agencies.

The shocking and treasonous actions of high-ranking government officials in the U.S. Department of Justice, FBI, CIA, NSA and other national security and intelligence services have done grave damage to our country.

In violation of their sworn oath to preserve, protect and defend the Constitution and laws of the United States, these vile criminals have acted instead to conspire against the American people, subvert their right to elect a President of their choosing, and devise a plot to remove the President from office by bearing false witness against him and others in his administration.

In plain terms, these traitors have attempted a coup d'état against the government of the United States and the American people. They must be brought to justice, prosecuted to the fullest extent of the law and held accountable.

All those who are found guilty of crimes against the United States or other felonies must be punished severely and sent to prison.

That includes those at the top.

We need intelligence agencies. We need the Department of Justice. And we need the Federal Bureau of Investigation. But we can never again allow any of them to engage in treason, abuses of power, bribery or schemes and actions that trample on the rights of the American people or that violate the laws or Constitution of the United States.

We need government agencies we can trust. Many employees at our intelligence agencies are hard-working patriots. But Deep State influence has pervaded these agencies at all levels. Corrupt officials and socialist ideologues should never be allowed to work in the Department of Justice, FBI or our national security and intelligence agencies — at any level.

Too much is at stake: Our national security, our liberty and our lives.

We must demand new leadership at all the federal departments where growing evidence of corruption and treason is being uncovered — at the DOJ, the FBI, the CIA and the NSA.

We need leaders who are honest, loyal, and patriotic Americans – not communists, community agitators and radicals open to treason and betrayal.

Tell President Trump and Congress to clean house!

The corruption is so all-pervasive and so dominant within the culture, that it's most probable that the best solution is to simply abolish the agencies and start from scratch with new employees, a smaller group of bureaucrats and a new spirit that can regain the American trust.

2. We must stop the Foreign Intelligence Surveillance Act (FISA) abuse.

As you read about in Chapter Five, the FISA law has opened the door to shocking abuses of power, by letting the federal government spy on the American people.

The FISA law includes procedures that allow the federal government to conduct physical and electronic surveillance of "foreign intelligence information" between "foreign powers" and "agents of foreign powers" suspected of espionage or terrorist conspiracies.

The FISA Law also created a Foreign Intelligence Surveillance Court to hear requests from federal law enforcement and intelligence agencies for secret surveillance warrants.

These warrants are intended to help disrupt and counter espionage conducted by foreign powers and to kill or capture terrorists before they can carry out their murderous plots against the United States and our allies.

Unfortunately, despite what may have been the best intentions of those who supported the FISA law — and the reassuring promises government officials made to the American people when it was enacted — that "genie is out of the bottle."

The FISA law has not stopped the federal government from spying on millions of Americans. In fact, despite repeated denials by high-ranking officials in the Obama administration, we now know that the NSA and other intelligence agencies collect massive amounts of information on virtually every U.S. citizen.

More recently, we have also learned that – as part of their ongoing conspiracy to remove President Trump from office – senior officials in the Department of Justice and FBI perpetrated a fraud on the U.S. Foreign Intelligence Surveillance Court by submitting contrived, false and sworn affidavits to the court that led to President Trump and his associates being wrongfully and illegally spied upon with the approval of President Barack Obama, Hillary Clinton and their co-conspirators.

These individuals, who suborned perjury and authorized others to commit outrageous violations of the law and our constitutional rights, may yet be held to account for their crimes.

In the United States of America, no one is above the law.

Many Americans believed that to be true, until Hillary Clinton ran for President – exposing "the tip of the iceberg" of corruption in our intelligence agencies and other government agencies.

It has been wisely said: "Power tends to corrupt, and absolute power corrupts absolutely." The FISA Court attests powerfully to that truth.

To put an end to the Deep State's creation of a Double Standard of Justice in America – one standard for the Clintons (and perhaps Barack Obama) and another standard for the rest of us – we must speak out against the FISA Law as currently written.

We must stiffen the penalties for bearing false testimony or committing perjury in the FISA Court – making each violation punishable as a 5-year minimum felony.

We must demand changes: Build a Cyber Wall that completely and for all time prevents any cyber violations of the Fourth Amendment to the U.S. Constitution and that protects all American citizens from unwarranted government intrusions into their lives, their property, their privacy and their thoughts.

3. We must demand that unnecessary departments be eliminated or significantly reduced in size.

The massive bureaucracy has created departments that are inefficient, ineffective and unnecessary – including, but not limited to, federal departments or agencies that should be:

Eliminated immediately…

- Commerce
- Housing and Urban Development
- Labor

- Small Business Administration

Returned to the states – or eliminated…

- Agriculture
- Education
- Energy
- Environmental Protection Agency
- Health and Human Services
- Interior
- Transportation

Departments like the U.S. Department of Education – which has effectively been turned into a National School Board of Deep State Busybodies and Progressive, Big Government, Anti-America Elitists – should be closed down immediately and its responsibilities should be returned to the individual states.

We should also put a full stop to any federal support for other taxpayer-funded progressive playpens like National Public Radio, Public Broadcasting System, National Endowment for the Arts, National Endowment for the Humanities and the Woodrow Wilson International Center for Scholars. These groups all claim to be progressive grownups. We should respect that claim and let them pay for their own ideologically driven causes and entertainment.

4. We must oppose the Deep State's "top down" approach.

The Deep State wants to take a top-down approach to maintain and expand their control. But we are a self-governing people.

We must oppose the Deep State's federal government programs and top-down rule over our lives. In America, the government derives its just powers from the consent of the governed. And we are endowed by

God with certain unalienable rights. Our rights do not come from government or the Deep State.

So, let's be very clear when we explain the Declaration of Independence and the U.S. Constitution to America's critics or enemies: Our rights do not come from the federal government or the Deep State. They are God-given and absolute.

5. We must always support and defend capitalism and free enterprise.

Only a free people, not government employees or the Deep State, can grow the economy and build wealth.

Only in a capitalist, free society can new businesses flourish and new ideas or innovators and risk-taking investors be rewarded with new wealth by freely creating and improving products and services purchased by customers in free, open and competitive markets.

Put simply, capitalism works best for everyone. Socialism destroys prosperity.

As Winston Churchill put it: "Some regard private enterprise as if it were a predatory tiger to be shot. Others look upon it as a cow that they can milk. Only a handful see it for what it really is — the strong horse that pulls the whole cart."[1]

Only when we are blessed with the abundance that capitalism makes possible can we best care for those among us who are truly in need. A free and private sector will always outperform the public sector — in efficiency, accountability and quality, and in producing increased wealth opportunity for all.

Final Thoughts

The curse of bureaucracy and socialism will never support an America that is free and prosperous.

A socialist agenda — the Deep State ideology — will always crush economic growth, waste dollars earned by America's hard-working taxpayers, corrupt government officials, and undermine the conservative, Judeo-Christian values upon which our constitutional republic was founded.

It's time to take a stand.

Each of us must resolve to fight the Deep State.

We must demand that the Deep State be exposed for what it is — a power-hungry, ideological agenda that is attempting to expand its power, grow itself, remain unaccountable and silence the voice of anyone who dares to oppose it.

Its appetite for power is insatiable. It has no moral compass but survival. It is the mortal enemy of our individual freedom and all that we hold dear as Americans.

As President Ronald Reagan said, "Freedom is never more than one generation away from extinction. We didn't pass it to our children in the bloodstream. It must be fought for, protected, and handed on for them to do the same."[2]

Now, we must take a stand, not only for our children, but for future generations — for our freedom and free enterprise, for our precious right to life, liberty and the pursuit of happiness, for a nation exceptional in human history, and for an America that is free and self-governing.

A Personal Statement

As you will probably know after reading this book, I am an ardent and steadfast champion of the U.S. Constitution, our limited and republican form of government, individual and religious liberty, equal justice under law, a free-market economic system, an intense and unceasing vigilance in protecting our freedoms and a strong national defense.

I believe that the United States of America is truly exceptional in human history, and that the principles enshrined in the Declaration of Independence and Constitution form – and remain — the unifying bedrock of our national and defining character as one nation, under God, indivisible, with liberty and justice for all.

As a Christian, I also believe and agree with the Declaration's proclamation that we are all created equal, that we are endowed by our Creator with certain unalienable rights, and that among these are life, liberty and the pursuit of happiness.

My Christian faith is also why I oppose abortion — and why I will always fight against the Deep State's culture of death and against the mass-extermination factories run by the depraved groups it supports, such as Planned Parenthood, which is still allowed to brutally kill unborn babies and receives money for their butchery from the federal government – that's you, the America taxpayer — to continue in their appalling barbarity.

I thank God that we still have the right to free speech in America and that we have the right to express the Christian belief that abortion is a monstrous crime against humanity.

Religious freedom has long been a central pillar of

our constitutional republic. In fact, the Bill of Rights and the First Amendment to the U.S. Constitution begins with the admonition to our government: "Congress shall make no law respecting an establishment of religion or prohibiting the free exercise thereof."

Like most Americans, I cherish those words, and the rights we enjoy in the exercise of religious faith – or no faith, as each individual sees fit – and the freedom to do so without government prohibition or interference.

We live in a world gripped by turmoil and wars — and in a country divided against itself. Today, crime, lawlessness, and violence are matters of serious and growing concern throughout America.

Unfortunately for America, many in the Deep State welcome the divisions in our country, the crime and the unchecked lawlessness that destroyed many of our once-great and prosperous urban areas.

Every American family should be able to live in peace and safety, and all of us should be confident that our laws and judicial system are fair.

I believe that the administration and enforcement of justice in America should be equal for all — impartial and objective — unyielding in respect for individual rights, liberty and due process as guaranteed by the Constitution of the United States and in accordance with the law.

I hope this book has helped you to gain a better understanding of the Deep State in America and the great danger it poses to our freedom and way of life.

Despite the menace that the Deep State represents, I am confident that the American people will again summon the strength and resolve — as they have always done in times of great moment or peril — to overcome and prevail against the shadowy government that is the Deep State.

As you and I work together to ensure that righteous victory, I pray that God will bless you, your loved ones and the United States of America.

Craig Huey

Deep State Book NOTES

Chapter ONE:

1. Huston, Warner Todd. "WASTE REPORT: Government Employees Cost U.S. $1 Million… EVERY MINUTE!" Constitution: Defending The Union from Threats Foreign and Domestic, 28 December 2017. https://constitution.com/waste-report-government-employees-cost-u-s-136-billion-every-minute/. April 2018.

2. Roberts, Hugh (16 July 2015). "The Hijackers [book review]". London Review of Books. 37 (14). Retrieved 7 August 2016.

3. Filkins, Dexter (12 March 2012). "Letter from Turkey. The Deep State". New Yorker. Retrieved 7 August 2016.

4. Eisenhower, Dwight D. "Military-Industrial Complex Speech." 1961. The Avalon Project. http://avalon.law.yale.edu/20th_century/eisenhower001.asp. April 2018.

5. Ibid.

Chapter TWO:

1. Will, George. "'Big Government' Is Ever Growing, on the Sly." National Review, 25 February 2017. https://www.nationalreview.com/2017/02/federal-government-growth-continues-while-federal-employee-numbers-hold/. April 2018.

2. Piaker, Zach. "Help Wanted: 4,000 Presidential Appointees." Partnership for Public Service Center for Presidential Transition, 16 March 2016. http://presidentialtransition.org/blog/posts/160316_help-wanted-4000-appointees.php. April 2018.

3. Meyer, Ali. "Porn-Watching EPA Employees Earning $120,000 A Year Put on Paid Administrative Leave." CNS News, 30 April 2015. https://www.cnsnews.com/news/article/ali-meyer/porn-watching-epa-employees-earning-120000-year-put-paid-administrative-leave. April 2018.

4. Dedaj, Paulina. "Deep state? 78 Obama appointees 'burrowed' in gov't, report says." Fox News Channel, 27 September 2017. http://www.foxnews.com/politics/2017/09/28/deep-state-78-obama-appointees-burrowed-in-govt-report-says.html. April 2018.

5. "Deep State – Shadow Government Revealed: Senior Executive Service." American Intelligence Media. https://aim4truth.org/2018/01/03/deep-state-shadow-government-revealed-senior-executive-service/. June 2018.

6. Star, Barbara. "Brennan: Officials should refuse to fire Mueller if asked to by Trump." CNN Politics, 21 July 2017. https://www.cnn.com/2017/07/21/politics/brennan-clapper-aspen-trump/index.html. April 2018.

7. Katz, Eric. "Critics Decry 'Propaganda' Posters in EPA Offices." Government Executive, 26 January 2018. https://www.govexec.com/federal-news/fedblog/2018/01/critics-decry-propoganda-posters-epa-offices/145497/. April 2018.

8. Wong, Kristina. "DEEP STATE: Trump Facing Seven Times More National Security Leaks Than Obama or Bush." Breitbart, 7 July 2017. http://www.breitbart.com/big-government/2017/07/07/deep-state-trump-facing-seven-times-more-national-security-leaks-than-obama-or-bush/. April 2018.

9. @ActualEPAFacts. "Hope Hicks (allegedly @realDonaldTrump's mistress) is a likely target for Mueller's investigation." https://twitter.com/search?q=altepa&src=typd.

10. @AltUSDA. "So Team Nunes is admitting that Papadopoulos triggered the FBI's Russia investigation – not the Steele dossier?" https://twitter.com/altusda.

11. @RogueNASA. https://www.facebook.com/RogueNASA/

Chapter THREE:

1. Goldfarb, Zachary A. and Karen Tumulty. "IRS admits targeting conservatives for tax scrutiny in 2012 election." The Washington Post, 10 May 2013. https://www.washingtonpost.com/business/economy/irs-admits-targeting-conservatives-for-tax-scrutiny-in-2013/05/10/3b6a0ada-b987-11e2-92f3-f291801936b8_story.html?noredirect=on&utm_term=.2705bb5da800. April 2018.

2. Watson, Kathryn. "Koskinen Denies IRS Still Targeting Conservatives Despite Contrary Court Ruling." The Daily Caller, 21 September 2016. http://dailycaller.com/2016/09/21/koskinen-denies-irs-still-targeting-conservatives-despite-contrary-court-ruling/. April 2018.

3. Ferrechio, Susan. "30,000 missing emails from IRS' Lerner recovered." Washington Examiner, 22 November 2014. https://www.washingtonexaminer.com/30-000-missing-emails-from-irs-lerner-recovered. April 2018.

4. Mooney, Chris and Brady Dennis." Extreme hurricanes and wildfires made 2017 the most costly U.S. disaster year on record." The Washington Post, 8 January 2018. https://www.washingtonpost.com/news/energy-environment/wp/2018/01/08/hurricanes-wildfires-made-2017-the-most-costly-u-s-disaster-year-on-record/?noredirect=on&utm_term=.c685f4399593. April 2018.

5. Taylor, Andrew. "House Overwhelmingly Passes $7.9 Billion Harvey Aid Bill." U.S. News, 6 September 2017. https://www.usnews.com/news/business/articles/2017-09-06/house-to-vote-on-79b-harvey-relief-bill. April 2018.

6. Bieszad, Andrew. "FEMA Gives Aid To Witch Shops And Strip Clubs After Hurricane Harvey But REFUSES To Help Christians, Says 'Churches Cannot Receive Taxpayer Help Because They Preach About Christ.'" Shoebat.com, 6 September 2017. http://shoebat.com/2017/09/06/fema-gives-aid-to-witch-shops-and-strip-clubs-after-hurricane-harvey-but-refuses-to-help-christians-says-churches-cannot-receive-taxpayer-help-because-they-preach-about-

christ/. April 2018.

7. Wallison, Peter J. "Four Years of Dodd-Frank Damage." The Wall Street Journal, 20 July 2014. https://www.wsj.com/articles/peter-wallison-four-years-of-dodd-frank-damage-1405893333. April 2018.

8. Miller, Brian. "The legacy of Mary Jo White." The Hill, 28 December 2016. http://thehill.com/blogs/pundits-blog/finance/312021-the-legacy-of-mary-jo-white. April 2018.

9. Temple-West, Patrick. "Corporate penalties have plunged at SEC since Trump took office." Politico, 27 October 2017. https://www.politico.com/story/2017/10/27/trump-sec-corporate-penalties-244239. April 2018.

10. Ibid.

11. "FY 2017 Department of Energy Budget Request Fact Sheet." Energy.gov. https://www.energy.gov/fy-2017-department-energy-budget-request-fact-sheet. April 2018.

12. Huston, Warner Todd. "WASTE REPORT: Government Employees Cost U.S. $1 Million… EVERY MINUTE!" Constitution: Defending The Union from Threats Foreign and Domestic, 28 December 2017. https://constitution.com/waste-report-government-employees-cost-u-s-136-billion-every-minute/. April 2018.

13. Jacobson, Louis. "Barack Obama says VA budget has risen 85 percent on his watch." Politifact, 30 September 2016. http://www.politifact.com/truth-o-meter/statements/2016/sep/30/barack-obama/barack-obama-says-va-budget-has-risen-85-percent-h/. April 2018.

14. Huston, Warner Todd. "WASTE REPORT: Government Employees Cost U.S. $1 Million… EVERY MINUTE!" Constitution: Defending The Union from Threats Foreign and Domestic, 28 December 2017. https://constitution.com/waste-report-government-employees-cost-u-s-136-billion-every-minute/. April 2018.

15. Devine, Curt. "307,000 veterans may have died awaiting Veterans Affairs health care, report says." CNN, 3 September 2015. https://www.cnn.com/2015/09/02/politics/va-inspector-general-report/index.html. April 2018.

16. Gomez, Jacy. "Remember the VA healthcare scandal? It's still happening" Washington Examiner, 31 October 2017. https://www.washingtonexaminer.com/remember-the-va-healthcare-scandal-its-still-happening. April 2018.

17. Devine Curt et al. "Report: Deadly delays in care continue at Phoenix VA." CNN, 4 October 2016. https://www.cnn.com/2016/10/04/politics/phoenix-va-deadly-delays-veterans/index.html. April 2018.

18. Malkin, Michelle. "Give VA Secretary David Shulkin the Boot." Creators, 7 March 2018. https://www.creators.com/read/michelle-malkin/03/18/give-va-secretary-david-shulkin-the-boot. May 2018.

19. Green, Emma. "Trump's Battle Over LGBT Discrimination Is Just

Beginning." The Atlantic, 28 July 2017. https://www.theatlantic.com/politics/archive/2017/07/title-vii/535182/. April 2018.

20. Sprigg, Peter. "Chai Feldblum Should Not Be Reappointed to the Equal Employment Opportunity Commission." Family Research Council, December 2017. https://downloads.frc.org/EF/EF17L44.pdf. April 2018.

21. Swann, Ben. "FDA's Disinformation Campaign on Kratom." Freedom Outpost, 24 February 2018. https://freedomoutpost.com/fdas-disinformation-campaign-kratom/. April 2018.

Chapter FOUR:

1. Lake, Rebecca. "How Much Income Puts You in the Top 1%, 5%, 10%?" Investopedia, 15 September 2016. https://www.investopedia.com/news/how-much-income-puts-you-top-1-5-10/. April 2018.

2. Jeffrey, Terence P. "Census Bureau: 4 Richest Counties in U.S. Are Suburbs of D.C." CNS News, 15 December 2016. https://www.cnsnews.com/news/article/terence-p-jeffrey/census-bureau-4-richest-counties-us-are-suburbs-dc. April 2018.

3. Loudenback, Tanya. "Middle-class Americans made more money last year than ever before." Business Insider, 12 September 2017. http://www.businessinsider.com/us-census-median-income-2017-9. June 2018.

4. Will, George. "'Big Government' Is Ever Growing, on the Sly." National Review, 25 February 2017. https://www.nationalreview.com/2017/02/federal-government-growth-continues-while-federal-employee-numbers-hold/. April 2018.

5. Huston, Warner Todd. "WASTE REPORT: Government Employees Cost U.S. $1 Million… EVERY MINUTE!" Constitution: Defending The Union from Threats Foreign and Domestic, 28 December 2017. https://constitution.com/waste-report-government-employees-cost-u-s-136-billion-every-minute/. April 2018.

6. Ibid.

7. Ibid.

8. Ibid.

9. Ibid.

10. Brown, Tim. "Why Is DC Withholding Salary Information for 255,000 Employees That You Pay For?" Freedom Outpost, 22 February 2018. https://freedomoutpost.com/dc-withholding-salary-information-255000-employees-pay/. April 2018.

11. Huston, Warner Todd. "WASTE REPORT: Government Employees Cost U.S. $1 Million… EVERY MINUTE!" Constitution: Defending The Union from Threats Foreign and Domestic, 28 December 2017. https://constitution.com/waste-report-government-employees-cost-u-s-136-billion-every-minute/.

April 2018.

12. Jacobs, Chris. "California's health insurance debacle." The Orange County Register, 21 December 2017. https://www.ocregister.com/2017/12/21/californias-health-insurance-debacle/. April 2018.

13. Ring, Edward. "California's Government Workers Make TWICE As Much as Private Sector Workers." California Policy Center, 24 January 2017. https://californiapolicycenter.org/californias-government-workers-make-twice-as-much-and-private-sector-workers/. April 2018.

14. Ashton, Adam and Phillip Reese. "California state payroll increased by $1 billion in 2017, twice as fast previous year." The Sacramento Bee, 20 January 2018. http://www.sacbee.com/news/politics-government/the-state-worker/article195655949.html. June 2018.

15. Ibid.

16. Kessler, Glen. "How many pages of regulations for 'Obamacare'?" The Washington Post, 15 May 2013. https://www.washingtonpost.com/blogs/fact-checker/post/how-many-pages-of-regulations-for-obamacare/2013/05/14/61eec914-bcf9-11e2-9b09-1638acc3942e_blog.html?utm_term=.c49ef8a01ff3. April 2018.

17. Ibid.

18. Westhill, Devon. "Regulating The Regulators, The 'Headless Fourth Branch.'" Investor's Business Daily, 19 December 2017. https://www.investors.com/politics/commentary/regulating-the-regulators-the-headless-fourth-branch/. April 2018.

19. Ibid.

20. "FedEx Corp. Reports First Quarter Earnings." FedEx. http://investors.fedex.com/news-and-events/investor-news/news-release-details/2017/FedEx-Corp-Reports-First-Quarter-Earnings/. April 2018.

21. "U.S. Postal Service Reports First Quarter 2018 Results." United States Postal Service. https://about.usps.com/news/national-releases/2018/pr18_012.htm April 2018.

22. "Postal Facts." United States Postal Service. http://facts.usps.com/size-and-scope/. April 2018.

23. Pociask, Steven. "A Failed Mission: U.S. Postal Service Details Another Massive Loss For The 2017 Fiscal Year." Forbes, 14 November 2017. https://www.forbes.com/sites/stevepociask/2017/11/14/a-failed-mission-u-s-postal-service-details-another-massive-loss-for-the-2017-fiscal-year/#75a6610b7f79. April 2018.

24. Ibid.

25. O' Brien, Mike. "President Trump Takes Aim at USPS, Amazon in Tweet." Multichannel Merchant, 2 January 2018. http://multichannelmerchant.com/operations/president-trump-takes-aim-usps-amazon-tweet/. April 2018.

26. LaRocco, Lori Ann. "The Truth About The Post Office's Financial Mess." CNBC, 24 October 2011. https://www.cnbc.com/id/45018432. April 2018.

27. McNicoll, Brian. "For every Amazon package it delivers, the Postal Service loses $1.46." Washington Examiner, 14 June 2018. https://www.washingtonexaminer.com/for-every-amazon-package-it-delivers-the-postal-service-loses-146. June 2018.

28. Ibarra, A. and Carmen Heredia Rodriguez. "California is outspending the U.S. government to market Obamacare." CNN Money, 3 December 2017. http://money.cnn.com/2017/12/03/news/economy/california-obamacare-marketing/index.html. April 2018.

29. "The World's Most Valuable Brands." Forbes. https://www.forbes.com/powerful-brands/list/#tab:rank. April 2018.

30. Am I The Only Techie Against Net Neutrality?" Forbes, 14 May 2014. https://www.forbes.com/sites/joshsteimle/2014/05/14/am-i-the-only-techie-againstnet-neutrality/#7956742f70d5. April 2018.

31. Ibid.

32. Rothschild, Mike. "The Biggest Military Wastes of Money." Ranker. https://www.ranker.com/list/biggest-military-wastes-of-money/mike-rothschild. April 2018.

Chapter FIVE:

1. German, Michael. "The US Intelligence Community Is Bigger Than Ever, But Is It Worth the Cost?" Defense One, 6 February 2015. https://www.defenseone.com/ideas/2015/02/us-intelligence-community-bigger-ever-it-worth-it/104799/. April 2018.

2. Bowden, John. "FBI agent in texts: 'We'll stop' Trump from becoming president." The Hill, 14 June 2018. http://thehill.com/policy/national-security/392284-fbi-agent-in-texts-well-stop-trump-from-becoming-president. June 2018.

3. Singman, Brooke. "FISA memo: Steele fired as an FBI source for breaking 'cardinal rule' --leaking to the media." Fox News, 2 February 2018. http://www.foxnews.com/politics/2018/02/02/fisa-memo-steele-fired-as-fbi-source-for-breaking-cardinal-rule-leaking-to-media.html. April 2018.

4. "Fusion GPS paid former British spy $168,000 to work on Trump dossier – report." CBS News, 2 November 2017. https://www.cbsnews.com/news/report-fusion-gps-paid-steele-168000-to-work-on-trump-dossier/. April 2018.

5. "Read the disputed memo here." CNN, 3 February 2018. https://www.cnn.com/2018/02/02/politics/fbi-nunes-memo-full/index.html. April 2018.

6. Pavlich, Katie. "BREAKING: DOJ Inspector General is Investigating James Comey for Potential Mishandling of Classified Information." Townhall, 18 June 2018. https://townhall.com/tipsheet/katiepavlich/2018/06/18/breaking-oig-is-investigating-james-comey-n2491947. June 2018.

7. Singman, Brooke. "FISA memo: Steele fired as an FBI source for breaking 'cardinal rule' --leaking to the media." Fox News, 2 February 2018. http://www.foxnews.com/politics/2018/02/02/fisa-memo-steele-fired-as-fbi-source-for-breaking-cardinal-rule-leaking-to-media.html. April 2018.

8. "Deep State Panic - Insider Information on Past, Present & Future Tactics." The Doug Hagmann Radio Show, August 2017. http://www.blogtalkradio.com/the-doug-hagmann-radio-show/2017/08/03/deep-state-panic--insider-information-on-past-present-future-tactics. April 2018/

9. Cawthorne, Cameron. "James Clapper: Intel Community 'Unmasked' 1,934 U.S. Persons in 2016." The Washington Free Beacon, 8 May 2017. http://freebeacon.com/national-security/james-clapper-intel-community-unmasked-1934-u-s-persons-2016/. April 2018.

10. Crowe, Jack. "Comey, Yates, McCabe, Rosenstein All Signed Off On Misleading FISA Apps." The Daily Caller, 2 February 2018. http://dailycaller.com/2018/02/02/comey-yates-mccabe-rosenstein-fisa/. April 2018.

11. Shane, Scott and Vindu Goel. "Fake Russian Facebook Accounts Bought $100,000 in Political Ads." The New York Times, 6 September 2017. https://www.nytimes.com/2017/09/06/technology/facebook-russian-political-ads.html. April 2018.

12. Constine, Josh. "Trump and Clinton spent $81M on US election Facebook ads, Russian agency $46K." TechCrunch, 1 November 2017. https://techcrunch.com/2017/11/01/russian-facebook-ad-spend/. April 2018.

13. "District of Columbia Results." The New York Times, 1 August 2017. https://www.nytimes.com/elections/results/district-of-columbia. April 2018.

14. Shortell, David. "Mueller attorney praised Yates as DOJ official, email shows." CNN Politics, 5 December 2017. https://www.cnn.com/2017/12/05/politics/mueller-emails-praise-doj-yates/index.html. April 2018.

15. Schallhorn, Kaitlyn. "Strzok, Page and the FBI texting scandal explained." Fox News, 27 April 2018. http://www.foxnews.com/politics/2018/04/27/strzok-page-and-fbi-texting-scandal-explained.html. April 2018.

16. Levine, Mike. "Senior FBI agent removed from Mueller's team repeatedly called Trump 'an idiot'." ABC News, 13 December 2017. http://abcnews.go.com/US/senior-fbi-agent-removed-muellers-team-repeatedly-called/story?id=51755829. April 2018.

17. Beavers, Olivia. "Dismissed FBI agent changed Comey's language on Clinton emails to 'extremely careless': report." The Hill, 4 December 2017. http://thehill.com/homenews/administration/363194-former-fbi-agent-changed-comeys-language-of-clinton-email-use-to. April 2018.

18. "My oh My, Latest Reports of FBI/DOJ Counterintelligence Operation Give Evelyn Farkas Statements New Light…" The Last Refuge, 26 December 2017. https://theconservativetreehouse.com/2017/12/26/my-oh-my-latest-reports-of-fbi-doj-counterintelligence-operation-evelyn-farkas-statements-take-on-new-light/. June 2018.

19. Ibid.

Chapter SIX:

1. Toobin, Jeffrey. "The Obama Brief." The New Yorker, 27 October 2014. https://www.newyorker.com/magazine/2014/10/27/obama-brief. April 2018.

2. https: Ibid.

3. Sessions, Jeff. "Attorney General Sessions Delivers Remarks on DACA." The United States Department of Justice, 5 September 2017. https://www.justice.gov/opa/speech/attorney-general-sessions-delivers-remarks-daca. April 2018.

4. Ibid.

5. Feuer, Alan. "Second Federal Judge Issues Injunction to Keep DACA in Place." The New York Times, 13 February 2018. https://www.nytimes.com/2018/02/13/nyregion/daca-dreamers-injunction-trump.html?mtrref=www.google.com&gwh=3174DB3E66C6DFEDF4BACDBF45E915E2&gwt=pay. April 2018

6. Carlson, Tucker. "Tucker: Federal courts the most decayed institution of all." Fox News Channel, 21 February 2018. https://www.youtube.com/watch?v=3SscKZXAdss. April 2018.

7. Olorunnipa, Toluse. "Trump Bans Transgender People From Military, Undoing Obama Move." Bloomberg Politics, 26 July 2017. https://www.bloomberg.com/news/articles/2017-07-26/trump-bans-transgender-americans-from-military-service. April 2018.

8. Lopez, German. "A federal court just blocked Trump's ban on transgender military service." Vox, 30 October 2017. https://www.vox.com/policy-and-politics/2017/10/30/16572580/court-trump-transgender-military-ban. April 2018.

9. "List of federal judges appointed by Donald Trump. Wikipedia. https://en.wikipedia.org/wiki/List_of_federal_judges_appointed_by_Donald_Trump. June 2018.

Chapter SEVEN:

1. "Hillary Clinton (D)) – 2016 Presidential Race." OpenSecrets.Org. https://www.opensecrets.org/pres16/candidate?id=n00000019. April 2018.

2. ibid.

3. ibid.

4. "Hillary Clinton: Contributions from Unions." https://www.unionfacts.com/pol/Hillary_Clinton_D/N00000019. June 2018.

5. Pearlstein, Joanna. "Techies Donate to Clinton in Droves. To Trump? Not So Much." Wired, 31 August 2016. https://www.wired.com/2016/08/techies-donate-clinton-droves-trump-not-much/. June 2018.

6. Allison, Bill et al. "Tracking the 2016 Presidential Money Race." Bloomberg Politics, 9 December 2016. https://www.bloomberg.com/politics/graphics/2016-presidential-campaign-fundraising/. April 2018.

7. Peek, Liz. "Obama's Auto Bailout Was Really a Hefty Union Payoff." The Fiscal Times, 17 October 2017. https://www.thefiscaltimes.com/Columns/2012/10/17/Obamas-Auto-Bailout-Was-Really-a-Hefty-Union-Payoff. April 2018.

8. Allen, Mike and David Rogers. "Bush announces $17.4 billion auto bailout." Politico, 19 December 2008. https://www.politico.com/story/2008/12/bush-announces-174-billion-auto-bailout-016740. April 2018.

9. "Bush approves $25 billion loan package for auto makers." Reuters, 30 September 2008. https://www.reuters.com/article/us-usa-congress-funding/bush-approves-25-billion-loan-package-for-auto-makers-idUSTRE48Q2WI20081001. April 2018.

10. Lawler, Joseph. "80 percent of taxpayers would get tax cuts next year under GOP bill, think tank says." Washington Examiner, 18 December 2017. https://www.washingtonexaminer.com/80-percent-of-taxpayers-would-get-tax-cuts-next-year-under-gop-bill-think-tank-says. April 2018.

11. Collinson, Stephen and Lauren Fox. "DC swamp creatures lie in wait for Trump's tax bill." CNN, 3 November 2017. https://www.cnn.com/2017/11/03/politics/trump-swamp-tax-reform/index.html. April 2018.

12. "Obamacare's $1 Trillion Tax Burden & Beyond." GOP, 22 March 2017. https://gop.com/obamacares-1-trillion-tax-burden-beyond?. April 2018.

13. Wayne, Alex. "Obamacare Website Costs Exceed $2 Billion, Study Finds." Bloomberg, 24 September 2014. https://www.bloomberg.com/news/articles/2014-09-24/obamacare-website-costs-exceed-2-billion-study-finds. April 2018.

14. Mercola, Joseph. "More Than Half of Americans Have Chronic Illnesses." Mercola, 30 November 2016. https://articles.mercola.com/sites/articles/archive/2016/11/30/expensive-us-health-care.aspx. April 2018.

15. "Mental Illness." National Institute of Mental Health. https://www.nimh.nih.gov/health/statistics/mental-illness.shtml. April 2018.

16. "U.S. Pharmaceutical Industry – Statistics & Facts." Statista. https://www.statista.com/topics/1719/pharmaceutical-industry/. April 2018.

17. Blumenthal, Paul and Dave Jamieson. "Koch Brothers Are Outspent By A Labor Force Millions Of Times Their Size, But..." Huffington Post, 15 March 2014. https://www.huffingtonpost.com/2014/03/15/kochs-brothers-labor_n_4966883.html. April 2018.

18. "Questions & Answers About AFSCME." American Federation of State, County & Municipal Employees. https://www.afscme.org/union/body/AFSCME-WMAH-QA-Booklet.pdf. April 2018.

19. Sherk, James. "F.D.R. Warned Us About Public Sector Unions." The New York

Times, 23 July 2014. https://www.nytimes.com/roomfordebate/2011/02/18/
the-first-blow-against-public-employees/fdr-warned-us-about-public-sector-
unions. April 2018.

20. Ibid.

21. Arnsdorf, Isaac. "Trump lobbying ban weakens Obama rules." Politico, 28
January 2017. https://www.politico.com/story/2017/01/trump-lobbying-ban-
weakens-obama-ethics-rules-234318. April 2018.

Chapter EIGHT:

1. Buncombe, Andrew. "Colin Powell says he'll vote for Hillary Clinton after
saying Donald Trump 'insults America every day.'" Independent, 25 October
2016. https://www.independent.co.uk/news/people/presidential-election-
colin-powell-vote-endorse-hillary-clinton-donald-trump-a7380226.html.
April 2018.

2. Calfas, Jennifer. "Trump Has Endorsed Mitt Romney. But Romney Once
Called Trump a 'Fraud' and Trump Said Romney 'Choked.'" Time, 20 February
2018. http://time.com/5166393/donald-trump-endorses-mitt-romney-twitter/.
April 2018.

3. Shays, Christopher. "Chris Shays: Why I'm voting for Hillary Clinton." CNN,
10 August 2016. https://www.cnn.com/2016/08/10/opinions/chris-shays-why-
im-voting-for-hillary-clinton/. April 2018.

4. Shaw, Adam. "Sen. Jeff Flake takes heat for 'absurd' speech comparing
Trump's press attacks to Stalin." Fox News. http://www.foxnews.com/
politics/2018/01/17/arizona-republican-sen-jeff-flake-blasts-trump-for-
attacks-on-press-in-fiery-senate-floor-speech.html.

5. Street, Chriss W. "Arnold Schwarzenegger, John Kasich to Launch 'New Way'
for California GOP." Breitbart, 28 February 2018. http://www.breitbart.com/
california/2018/02/28/schwarzenegger-ohios-gov-kasich-join-trans-gop-new-
way-california/. April 2018.

Chapter NINE:

1. McGovern, Shannon. "The Real Threat From Money In Politics Comes
From the Left." U.S. News, 27 June 2012. https://www.usnews.com/opinion/
articles/2012/06/27/the-real-threat-from-money-in-politics-comes-from-the-
left. April 2018.

2. del Guidice, Rachel. "Unions Give More Than $1.1 Billion to Democrats,
Liberal Groups." The Daily Signal, 5 January 2018. https://www.dailysignal.
com/2018/01/05/unions-gave-more-than-1-1-billion-to-democrats-liberal-
groups/. April 2018.

3. Henke, John. "Liberal Foundations Get Almost No Coverage Despite Spending
Insane Amounts of Money on Politics." Bold, 23 January 2016. https://bold.
global/jon-henke/2016/01/23/liberal-foundations-get-almost-no-coverage-

despite-spending-insane-amounts-of-money-on-politics/. April 2018.

4. "Billionaires back Black Lives Matter." World Socialist Web Site, 11 October 2016. https://www.wsws.org/en/articles/2016/10/11/pers-o11.html. April 2018.

5. McGovern, Shannon. "The Real Threat From Money In Politics Comes From the Left." U.S. News, 27 June 2012. https://www.usnews.com/opinion/articles/2012/06/27/the-real-threat-from-money-in-politics-comes-from-the-left. April 2018.

6. "Where Does the ACLU Get Its Money?" Fox News, 7 January 2003. http://www.foxnews.com/story/2003/01/07/where-does-aclu-get-its-money.html. April 2018.

7. "Company Overview of The Pew Charitable Trusts" Bloomberg. https://www.bloomberg.com/research/stocks/private/snapshot.asp?privcapId=3534933. April 2018.

8. Bosilkovski, Igor. "After Big Gift, George Soros' Fortune Shrinks, Knocking Him Down The Forbes List." Forbes, 19 October 2017. https://www.forbes.com/sites/igorbosilkovski/2017/10/19/after-big-gift-george-soros-fortune-more-than-halved-falls-40-spots-on-rich-list-ck/#35c8d3ea21ee. April 2018.

9. "Alliance for Justice." Activist Facts. https://www.activistfacts.com/?s=alliance+for+justice.

10. Ibid.

11. Ibid.

12. Henke, John. "Liberal Foundations Get Almost No Coverage Despite Spending Insane Amounts of Money on Politics." Bold, 23 January 2016. https://bold.global/jon-henke/2016/01/23/liberal-foundations-get-almost-no-coverage-despite-spending-insane-amounts-of-money-on-politics/. April 2018.

13. Ibid.

14. Henke, John. "How Left-Wing Foundations Control Politics." The American Spectator, 16 May 2016. https://spectator.org/foundations-and-politics-how-left-wing-foundations-dominate-the-game/. April 2018.

15. "Natural Resources Defense Council." Big Green Radicals. https://www.biggreenradicals.com/group/natural-resources-defense-council/. April 2018.

16. Ibid.

17. Ibid.

18. "Natural Resources Defense Council." Influence Watch. https://www.influencewatch.org/non-profit/natural-resources-defense-council-nrdc/. April 2018.

19. "The California Endowment: Los Angeles Grants." Inside Philanthropy. https://www.insidephilanthropy.com/fundraising-los-angeles-grants/the-california-endowment-los-angeles-grants.html. April 2018.

Chapter TEN:

1. Ebeling, Paul. "Barack Hussein Obama is Still Intent in Destroying America." Live Trading News, 10 September 2017. http://www.livetradingnews.com/barack-hussein-obama-still-intent-destroying-america-54415.html#.Wuj2KGXyruR. April 2018.

2. Vadum, Matthew. "Organizing for Anarchy." Frontpage Mag, 18 July 2017. https://www.frontpagemag.com/fpm/267308/organizing-anarchy-matthew-vadum. April 2018.

3. Sperry, Paul. "How Obama is scheming to sabotage Trump's presidency." New York Post, 11 February 2017. https://nypost.com/2017/02/11/how-obama-is-scheming-to-sabotage-trumps-presidency/. April 2018.

4. Aley, James. "Wall Street's King Quant David Shaw's Secret Formulas Pile Up Money. Now He Wants a Piece of the Net." Fortune Magazine, 5 February 1996. http://archive.fortune.com/magazines/fortune/fortune_archive/1996/02/05/207353/index.htm. April 2018.

5. "Organizing for Action: Who's Giving to Obama-Linked Nonprofit?" Open Secrets Org, 17 June 2014. https://www.opensecrets.org/news/2014/06/organizing-for-action-whos-giving-to-obama-linked-nonprofit/. April 2018.

6. Ibid.

7. Ibid.

8. Ibid.

9. "Obama's Approval Rating Drops to Lowest Ever, According to Gallup." Fox News, 14 August 2011. http://www.foxnews.com/politics/2011/08/14/obamas-approval-rating-drops-to-lowest-ever-according-to-gallup.html. April 2018.

10. Ibid.

11. Memoli, Michael A. "In California, a test run for the Obama campaign." Los Angeles Times, 13 July 2011. http://articles.latimes.com/2011/jul/13/news/la-pn-obama-hahn-20110713. June 2018.

12. Robillard, Kevin. "Study: Youth vote was decisive." Politico, 7 November 2012. https://www.politico.com/story/2012/11/study-youth-vote-was-decisive-083510. April 2018.

Chapter ELEVEN:

1. Snead, Jason. "Why Dissolving the Election Fraud Commission Is a True Loss for the Nation." The Daily Signal, 5 January 2018. https://www.dailysignal.com/2018/01/05/379558/. April 2018.

2. Ibid.

3. Weston, Ethan. "11 California Counties Might Have More Registered Voters Than Eligible." ABC Channel 2 News, 6 August 2017. https://www.wmar2news.com/newsy/11-california-counties-might-have-more-registered-voters-than-eligible. April 2018.

4. Scarborough, Rowan. "Nearly 2 million non-citizen Hispanics illegally registered to vote." The Washington Times, 15 February 2017. https://www. washingtontimes.com/news/2017/feb/15/nearly-2-million-non-citizen-hispanics-illegally-r/. April 2018.

5. Frank, Stephen. "Poll: 13% of Illegal Aliens ADMIT They Vote—2015 Report." California Political Review, 26 January 2017. http://www.capoliticalreview. com/capoliticalnewsandviews/poll-13-of-illegal-aliens-admit-they-vote-2015-report/. April 2018.

6. Snead, Jason. "Why Dissolving the Election Fraud Commission Is a True Loss for the Nation." The Daily Signal, 5 January 2018. https://www.dailysignal. com/2018/01/05/379558/. April 2018.

7. "California Secretary of State Alex Padilla Statement on Dissolution of President's Voter Fraud Commission." Alex Padilla California Secretary of State. 3 January 2018. http://www.sos.ca.gov/administration/news-releases-and-advisories/2018-news-releases-and-advisories/california-secretary-state-alex-padilla-statement-dissolution-presidents-voter-fraud-commission/. June 2018.

8. Lucas, Fred. "More Than 800,000 Noncitizens May Have Voted in 2016 Election, Expert Says." The Daily Signal, 28 November 2017. https://www. dailysignal.com/2016/11/28/more-than-800000-noncitizens-could-have-voted-in-2016-election-experts-say/. April 2018.

9. Lucas, Fred. "More Than 800,000 Noncitizens May Have Voted in 2016 Election, Expert Says." The Daily Signal, 28 November 2017. https://www. dailysignal.com/2016/11/28/more-than-800000-noncitizens-could-have-voted-in-2016-election-experts-say/. April 2018.

10. Schoffstall, Joe. "More Than 7 Million Voter Registrations Are Duplicated in Multiple States." The Washington Free Beacon, 18 May 2017. http:// freebeacon.com/issues/7-million-voter-registrations-duplicated-multiple-states/. April 2018.

11. Schinella, Tony. "Nearly 95K Voters In NH Registered In Other States: Data." Concord Patch, 31 May 2017. https://patch.com/new-hampshire/concord-nh/ nearly-95k-voters-nh-registered-other-states-data. April 2018.

12. Von Spakovsky, Hans. "New Report Exposes Thousands of Illegal Votes in 2016 Election." The Daily Signal, 28 July 2017. https://www.dailysignal. com/2017/07/28/new-report-exposes-thousands-illegal-votes-2016-election/. April 2018.

13. York, Byron. "York: When 1,099 felons vote in race won by 312 ballots." Washington Examiner, 6 August 2018. https://www.washingtonexaminer. com/york-when-1099-felons-vote-in-race-won-by-312-ballots/ article/2504163. April 2018.

14. "U.S. unauthorized immigration population estimates." Pew Research Center, 3 November 2016. http://www.pewhispanic.org/interactives/unauthorized-immigrants/. April 2018.

15. Underhill, Wendy. "Voter Identification Requirements/Voter ID Laws." National Conference of State Legislatures, 5 January 2018. http://www.ncsl. org/research/elections-and-campaigns/voter-id.aspx. April 2018.

Chapter TWELVE:

1. Philipp, Joshua. "'Deep State' Exposed in New Report." The Epoch Times, 7 September 2017. https://www.theepochtimes.com/deep-state-exposed-in-new-report_2293459.html. April 2018.

2. Katz, Josh. "Who Will Be President?" The New York Times, 8 November 2016. https://www.nytimes.com/interactive/2016/upshot/presidential-polls-forecast. html. April 2018.

3. Bannister, Craig. "Study: 90% of Network Coverage of President Trump Negative in 2017." CNS News, 16 January 2018. https://www.cnsnews.com/ blog/craig-bannister/study-90-networks-trump-coverage-negative-2017. April 2018.

4. "Trump Gets under the Media's Spin." Family Research Council, 13 December 2017. https://www.frc.org/updatearticle/20171213/media-spin. May 2018.

5. Ingram, Mathew. "TV Watching Is in Decline, But News Consumption Is Booming." Fortune, 3 April 2017. http://fortune.com/2017/04/03/nielsen-news-report/. April 2018.

6. Noyes, Rich and Mike Ciandella. "2017: The Year the News Media Went to War Against a President." MRC NewsBusters, 16 January 2018. https://www. newsbusters.org/blogs/nb/rich-noyes/2018/01/16/2017-year-news-media-went-war-against-president. May 2018.

7. Cineas, Fabiola. "Todd Carmichael: Trump's Tax Plan Will Destroy the Middle Class." Philadelphia, 28 November 2017. https://www.phillymag.com/ business/2017/11/28/todd-carmichael-trump-tax-plan-middle-class/. May 2018.

8. Long, Heather. "The average American family will get $4,000 from tax cuts, Trump team claims." The Washington Post, 16 October 2017. https://www.washingtonpost.com/news/wonk/wp/2017/10/16/the-average-american-family-will-get-4000-from-tax-cuts-trump-team-claims/?noredirect=on&utm_term=.419eba9e6c28. May 2018.

9. Merline, John. "Has Anyone Noticed That Trump's Economy Keeps Beating Expectations?" Investor's Business Daily, 7 December 2017. https:// www.investors.com/politics/commentary/trump-economy-gdp-growth-unemployment/. May 2018.

10. Gillespie, Patrick and Chris Isidore. "U.S. unemployment drops to lowest in 17 years." CNN, 3 November 2017. http://money.cnn.com/2017/11/03/news/ economy/october-jobs-report/index.html. May 2018.

11. La Monica, Paul R. "Black unemployment rate hits a record low." CNN Money, June 1 2018. http://money.cnn.com/2018/06/01/news/economy/ black-unemployment-rate-record-low/index.html. June 2018.

12. DeMarche, Edmund et al. "North Korea agrees to 'complete denuclearization of the Korean Peninsula' after Trump-Kim summit." Fox News, 12 June 2018. http://www.foxnews.com/politics/2018/06/12/trump-kim-jong-un-sign-comprehensive-document-vague-on-specific-details.html. June 2018.

13. @Newsweek. "Trump bars Americans on Twitter but tells Iran to unblock social media sites." 2 January 2018. https://twitter.com/newsweek/status/948307936660672512?lang=en. May 2018.

14. Ha, Thu-Huong. "Amazon just deleted over 900 reviews of Hillary Clinton's new book." 13 September 2017. https://qz.com/1076357/hillary-clintons-what-happened-amazon-just-deleted-over-900-reviews-of-hillary-clintons-new-book/. May 2018.

Chapter THIRTEEN:

1. Maza, Cristina. "Christian Persecution and Genocide Worse Now than 'Any Time in History,' Report Says." Newsweek, 4 January 2018. http://www.newsweek.com/christian-persecution-genocide-worse-ever-770462. June 2018.

2. "FACT SHEET: Obama Administration's Record and the LGBT Community." The White House, President Barack Obama, 9 June 2016. https://obamawhitehouse.archives.gov/the-press-office/2016/06/09/fact-sheet-obama-administrations-record-and-lgbt-community. May 2018.

3. Ibid.

4. "Religious Landscape Study." Pew Research Center. http://www.pewforum.org/religious-landscape-study/. May 2018.

5. "United States Population 2018." World Population Review. http://worldpopulationreview.com/countries/united-states-population/. May 2018.

6. "Elane Photography v. Willock." Alliance Defending Freedom. https://www.adflegal.org/detailspages/case-details/elane-photography-v.-willock. May 2018.

7. Valens, Ana. "How big is the transgender population, really?" The Daily Dot, 13 June 2017. https://www.dailydot.com/irl/transgender-population-in-us/. May 2018.

8. Kliff, Sarah. "Planned Parenthood gets over $500 million annually in public funds. Here's where it goes." Vox, 26 July 2016. https://www.vox.com/2015/7/22/9013565/planned-parenthood-government-funding. May 2018.

9. "The Real Planned Parenthood: Leading the Culture of Death." Family Research Council. https://downloads.frc.org/EF/EF15F70.pdf. May 2018.

Chapter FOURTEEN:

1. Frederic Bastiat "What Is Seen and What Is Not Seen", Selected Essays on Political Economy, Foundation for Economic Education, Page 13, 1995

2. Hartzler, Vicky (R-MO). "Solving one of Reagan's 'problems.'" The Hill. http://thehill.com/blogs/congress-blog/economy-budget/285972-solving-one-of-reagans-problems. June 2018.

3. Weinberger, David. "Friedrich von Hayek: The Road to Serfdom." 14 June 2010. https://www.dailysignal.com/2010/06/14/friedrich-von-hayek-the-road-to-serfdom/. June 2018.

4. "Milton Friedman in Capitalism and Freedom." http://www.ontheissues.org/Archive/Capitalism_Freedom_Milton_Friedman.htm. June 2018.

Chapter FIFTEEN:

1. " 'Socialism is the philosophy of failure...' – Winston Churchill." The Churchill Project, 30 July 2015. https://winstonchurchill.hillsdale.edu/socialism-is-the-philosophy-of-failure-winston-churchill/. June 2018.

2. "Americans Favor Capitalism, Tempted By Socialism, Ill-Informed About Both." American Culture & Faith Institute. https://www.culturefaith.com/americans-favor-capitalism-temoted-by-socialism/. June 2018.

3. Friedman, Milton. "American Economist." Think Exist. http://thinkexist.com/quotation/nobody-spends-somebody-else-s-money-as-carefully/386829.html. June 2018.

4. Holodny, Elena. "87% of Venezuelans say they don't have money to buy enough food." Business Insider, 20 June 2016. https://www.businessinsider.in/87-of-Venezuelans-say-they-dont-have-money-to-buy-enough-food/articleshow/52842091.cms. June 2018.

5. D'Amato, Pete. "Being the ex-President's daughter pays off: Hugo Chavez's ambassador daughter is Venezuela's richest woman." DailyMail.com, 10 August 2015. http://www.dailymail.co.uk/news/article-3192933/Hugo-Chavez-s-ambassador-daughter-Venezuela-s-richest-woman-according-new-report.html. June 2018.

EPILOGUE:

1. "Winston S. Churchill: Quotes." https://www.goodreads.com/quotes/74850-some-regard-private-enterprise-as-if-it-were-a-predatory. June 2018.

2. "Ronald Reagan and Federalism." Reagan Foundation. http://home.reaganfoundation.org/site/DocServer/ReaganMomentsFebEssay_-_Federalism.pdf?docID=587. June 2018.

Deep State Additional Sources

Chapter ONE:

Wills, Matthew. "The Turkish Origins of the 'Deep State.'" JSTOR Daily, 10 April 2017. https://daily.jstor.org/the-unacknowledged-origins-of-the-deep-state/. June 2018.

Roberts, Hugh (16 July 2015). "The Hijackers [book review]". London Review of Books. 37 (14). Retrieved 7 August 2016.

Filkins, Dexter (12 March 2012). "Letter from Turkey. The Deep State". New Yorker. Retrieved 7 August 2016.

Chapter TWO:

Restuccia, Andrew et al. "Federal workers turn to encryption to thwart Trump." Politico, 2 February 2017. https://www.politico.com/story/2017/02/federal-workers-signal-app-234510. April 2018.

Loris, Nicolas. "The Many Problems of the EPA's Clean Power Plan and Climate Regulations: A Primer." The Heritage Foundation, 7 July 2015. https://www.heritage.org/environment/report/the-many-problems-the-epas-clean-power-plan-and-climate-regulations-primer. April 2018.

Farivar, Cyrus. "House members: EPA officials may be using Signal to 'spread their goals covertly.'" ARS Technica, 15 February 2017. https://arstechnica.com/tech-policy/2017/02/house-members-epa-officials-may-be-using-signal-to-spread-their-goals-covertly/. April 2018.

"Complying with President Trump's Executive Order on Energy Independence - President signs the order on March 28." United States Environmental Protection Agency. https://www.epa.gov/energy-independence. April 2018.

"Obama planning to sidestep Congress for next phase in climate change agenda." Fox News Politics, 25 June 2013. http://www.foxnews.com/politics/2013/06/25/obama-will-reportedly-introduce-new-carbon-emissions-rules-in-climate-change.html. April 2018.

Loris, Nicolas. "The Many Problems of the EPA's Clean Power Plan and Climate Regulations: A Primer." The Heritage Foundation, 7 July 2015. https://www.heritage.org/environment/report/the-many-problems-the-epas-clean-power-plan-and-climate-regulations-primer. April 2018.

Follett, Andrew. "Top 11 Problems Plaguing Solar And Wind Power." 25 December 2017. http://dailycaller.com/2015/12/25/top-11-problems-plaguing-solar-and-wind-power/. April 2018.

Timmer, John. "In killing the Clean Power Plan, EPA wants a narrow Clean Air Act." ARS Technica, 10 October 2017. https://arstechnica.com/science/2017/10/in-killing-the-clean-power-plan-epa-wants-a-narrow-clean-air-act/. April 2018.

Jarrett, Terry M. "EPA's Clean Power Plan oversteps federal authority." St. Louis Post-Dispatch, 13 November 2015. http://www.stltoday.com/opinion/columnists/epa-s-clean-power-plan-oversteps-federal-authority/article_67b946eb-c24e-561d-b61e-245aaa7a3ebd.html. May 2018.

Kreutzer, David. "Another Useless EPA Regulation That'll Cost Americans More Money." The Heritage Foundation, 3 December 2015. https://www.heritage.org/environment/commentary/another-useless-epa-regulation-thatll-cost-americans-more-money. April 2018.

Cama, Timothy. "Energy Dept refuses to name staffers who worked on climate." The Hill, 13 December 2016. http://thehill.com/policy/energy-environment/310133-energy-dept-wont-give-climate-change-staffers-names-to-trump. April 2018.

Epstein, Richard A. "Junk Obama's Clean Power Plan." Hoover Institution, 30 October 2017. https://www.hoover.org/research/junk-obamas-clean-power-plan. April 2018.

Toosi, Nahal, and Andrew Restuccia. "Trump plans to sign order keeping Gitmo open, leaked doc reveals." Politico, 25 January 2018. https://www.politico.com/story/2018/01/25/trump-guantanamo-gitmo-leaked-document-369687. April 2018.

Mclaughlin, Kelly. "Is the Pentagon trying to undermine Trump? Department of Defense tweets about Iraqi refugee who became a Marine on the same day President bans immigrants from seven Muslim countries." Daily Mail, 26 January 2017. http://www.dailymail.co.uk/news/article-4159378/Department-Defense-tweets-refugee-Marine.html. April 2018.

Chapter THREE:

Shelley, Susan. "IRS targeting settlement as scary as the scandal." Los Angeles Daily News, 15 December 2017. https://www.dailynews.com/2017/12/15/irs-targeting-settlement-as-scary-as-the-scandal/. April 2018.

Spiering, Charles. "Congressman: IRS asked pro-life group about 'the content of their prayers.'" Washington Examiner, 17 May 2013. https://www.washingtonexaminer.com/congressman-irs-asked-pro-life-group-about-the-content-of-their-prayers. April 2018.

Williamson, Elizabeth. "Agency Official Behind Firestorm." The Wall Street Journal, 14May 2013. https://www.wsj.com/articles/SB100014241278873240314045 78483513309383922. April 2018.

"IRS Scandal Fast Facts." CNN, 1 October 2017. https://www.cnn. com/2014/07/18/politics/irs-scandal-fast-facts/index.html. April 2018.

Boyle, John. "Graham says IRS targeted his non-profits with audits." USA Today, 16 May 2013. https://www.usatoday.com/story/news/nation/2013/05/16/franklin-graham-nonprofits-irs-audits/2165647/. April 2018.

Wyland, Michael. "Whatever Happened to the IRS Tax Exemption Scandal?" Nonprofit Quarterly, 22 August 2017. https://nonprofitquarterly.org/2017/08/22/whatever-happened-irs-tax-exemption-scandal/. April 2018.

Tankersley, Jim. "To Lead I.R.S., Trump Nominates Lawyer Who Battled It." The New York Times, 8 February 2018. https://www.nytimes.com/2018/02/08/politics/charles-rettig-irs-commissioner.html. April 2018.

Bastach, Michael. "Congress Accuses EPA Chief Of Lying, Mentions Criminal Prosecution." The Daily Caller, 13 August 2015. http://dailycaller.com/2015/08/13/congress-accuses-epa-chief-of-lying-mentions-criminal-prosecution/. April 2018.

Bastach, Michael. "EPA Grants Itself Power To Regulate Ponds, Ditches, Puddles." The Daily Caller, 27 May 2015. http://dailycaller.com/2015/05/27/epa-grants-itself-power-to-regulate-ponds-ditches-puddles/. April 2018.

Bakst, Daren. "Trump Is Repealing Obama's Harmful Water Rule. Why Efforts to Stop Him Are Misguided." The Daily Signal, 2 February 2018. https://www.dailysignal.com/2018/02/02/trump-repealing-obamas-harmful-water-rule-efforts-stop-misguided/. April 2018.

Mooney, Chris et al. "Trump names Scott Pruitt, Oklahoma attorney general suing EPA on climate change, to head the EPA." The Washington Post, 8 December 2016. https://www.washingtonpost.com/news/energy-environment/wp/2016/12/07/trump-names-scott-pruitt-oklahoma-attorney-general-suing-epa-on-climate-change-to-head-the-epa/?noredirect=on&utm_term=.836ac0561984. April 2018.

Fernandez, Manny et al. "Still Waiting for FEMA in Texas and Florida After Hurricanes." The New York Times, 22 October 2017. https://www.nytimes.com/2017/10/22/us/fema-texas-florida-delays-.html. April 2018.

Penton, Kevin. "FEMA denies aid to religious groups hit by Sandy." USA Today, 25 July 2013. https://www.usatoday.com/story/news/nation/2013/07/25/fema-denies-aid-to-religious-groups-hard-hit-by-sandy-/2588519/. April 2018.

Boorstein, Michelle. "In a shift, Trump administration says houses of worship can apply for FEMA funding for Hurricane Harvey relief." The Washington Post, 9 January 2018. https://www.washingtonpost.com/news/acts-of-faith/wp/2018/01/04/in-a-shift-trump-administration-says-houses-of-worship-can-get-direct-fema-funding-after-disasters/?noredirect=on&utm_term=.b57b-8405f04b. April 2018.

"Equal Access: Trump administration reverses rule, allows churches access to FEMA disaster relief." Texarkana Gazette, 21 January 2018. http://www.texarkanagazette.com/news/opinion/editorials/story/2018/jan/21/equal-access-trump-administration-reverses-rule-allows-churches-access-fema-disaster-relief/709658/. April 2018.

Cama, Timothy. "Trump seeks to cut Energy Department loan, research programs." The Hill, 12 February 2018. http://thehill.com/policy/energy-environment/373429-trump-seeks-to-cut-energy-dept-loan-research-programs. April 2018.

DiChristopher, Tom. "Regulators reject Energy Secretary Rick Perry's plan to subsidize coal and nuclear plants." CNBC, 8 January 2018. https://www.cnbc.com/2018/01/08/regulators-reject-rick-perrys-plan-to-prop-up-coal-and-nuclear-plants.html. April 2018.

Walsh, Steve et al. "VA Hospitals Still Struggling With Adding Staff Despite Billions From Choice Act." NPR, 31 January 2017. https://www.npr.org/2017/01/31/512052311/va-hospitals-still-struggling-with-adding-staff-despite-billions-from-choice-act. April 2018.

Fahrentold, David. "How the VA developed its culture of coverups." The Washington Post, 30 May 2014. http://www.washingtonpost.com/sf/national/2014/05/30/how-the-va-developed-its-culture-of-coverups/?utm_term=.fac1e10efe92. April 2018.

"What You Should Know About EEOC and the Enforcement Protections for LGBT Workers." U.S. Equal Employment Opportunity Commission. https://www.eeoc.gov/eeoc/newsroom/wysk/enforcement_protections_lgbt_workers.cfm. April 2018.

Chapter FOUR:

"FLYTENOW V. FAA." Goldwater Institute. https://goldwaterinstitute.org/flytenow-v-faa/. April 2018.

Zhao, Helen. "Union heavyweight wants to ban UPS from using drones or driverless vehicles." CNBC, 24 January 2018. https://www.cnbc.com/2018/01/24/labor-teamsters-want-to-ban-ups-from-using-drones-driverless-vehicles.html. April 2018.

Palladino, Valentina. "Amazon to take on UPS, FedEx via 'Shipping with Amazon'." ARS Technica, 9 February 2018. https://arstechnica.com/information-technology/2018/02/amazon-to-take-on-ups-fedex-via-shipping-with-amazon/. April 2018.

Gutierrez, Melody. "California's $400 billion debt worries analysts." San Francisco Chronicle, 6 February 2016. https://www.sfchronicle.com/politics/article/California-s-400-billion-debt-worries-analysts-6812264.php. April 2018.

Chapter FIVE:

Scallhorn, Kaitlyn. "FISA surveillance program: What is it and why is it so controversial?" Fox News. http://www.foxnews.com/politics/2018/01/19/fisa-surveillance-program-what-is-it-and-why-is-it-so-controversial.html. April 2018.

Jackson, Nate. "FBI: Deep-State Collusion." The Patriot Post, 8 December 2017. https://patriotpost.us/articles/52825-fbi-deep-state-collusion. April 2018.

Gallatin, Thomas. "Growing Stench of Politics Rising From Team Mueller." The Patriot Post, 13 December 2017. https://patriotpost.us/articles/52913-growing-stench-of-politics-rising-from-team-mueller. April 2018.

Bensinger, Ken. "These Reports Allege Trump Has Deep Ties To Russia." BuzzFeed News, 10 January 2017. https://www.buzzfeed.com/kenbensinger/these-reports-allege-trump-has-deep-ties-to-russia?utm_term=.kxM0PBYLv0#.nnWO-5QvprO. April 2018.

Volz, Dustin. "Justice Department affirms no evidence Obama wiretapped Trump." Reuters, 2 September 2017. https://www.reuters.com/article/us-usa-trump-surveillance/justice-department-affirms-no-evidence-obama-wiretapped-trump-idUSKCN1BD0UO. April 2018.

Chavez, Michael Robinson. "Reports: Paul Manafort was wiretapped, has been told to expect an indictment." Vox, 19 September 2017. https://www.vox.com/2017/9/18/16330978/paul-manafort-wiretap-indictment. April 2018.

Schwartz, Ian. "Tucker Carlson: The Obama Administration Spied On A Rival Political Campaign." Real Clear Politics, 10 February 2018. https://www.realclearpolitics.com/video/2018/02/10/tucker_carlson_the_obama_administration_spied_on_a_rival_political_campaign.html. April 2018.

Pandolfo, Chris. "Mueller investigator previously defended Clinton IT staffer." Conservative Review, 8 December 2017. https://www.conservativereview.com/articles/mueller-investigator-previously-defended-clinton-it-staffer/. April 2018.

Shaw, Adam and Brooke Singman. "DOJ IG releases explosive report that led to firing of ex-FBI Deputy Director Andrew McCabe." Fox News. http://www.foxnews.com/politics/2018/04/13/doj-ig-releases-explosive-report-that-led-to-firing-ex-fbi-deputy-director-andrew-mccabe.html. April 2018.

Timmerman, Kenneth. "Democrat's FISA memo doesn't refute GOP charges." The Hill, 26 February 2018. http://thehill.com/opinion/white-house/375560-democrats-fisa-memo-doesnt-refute-gop-charges. April 2018.

Brandon, Alex. "FBI disciplinary office recommends firing former deputy director Andrew McCabe." Los Angeles Times, 14 March 2018. http://www.latimes.com/politics/la-na-pol-justice-department-mccabe-fbi-20180314-story.html. May 2018.

Cheney, Kyle and Aubree Eliza Weaver. "DOJ, House GOP lurch toward confrontation in document fight." Politico, 17 June 2018. https://www.politico.com/story/2018/06/17/gowdy-fbi-rosenstein-wray-mccabe-650395. June 2018.

Chapter SEVEN:

Cancryn, Adam et al. "Deep-pocketed health care lobbies line up against Trump." Politico, 3 May 2017. https://www.politico.com/story/2017/05/03/obamacare-repeal-health-care-237948. April 2018.

Bienenstock, David. "Big Pharma Wants a Monopoly In One of Weed's Key Medicinal Compounds." Motherboard, 13 June 2017. https://motherboard.vice.com/en_us/article/wjqp5n/big-pharma-wants-a-monopoly-on-one-of-weeds-key-medicinal-compounds-nd. April 2018.

McGinty, Tom and Brody Mullins. "Political Spending by Unions Far Exceeds Direct Donations." The Wall Street Journal, 10 July 2017. https://www.wsj.com/articles/SB10001424052702304782404577488584031850026. April 2018.

Sherk, James. "Majority of Union Members Now Work for the Government." The Heritage Foundation, 22 January 2010. https://www.heritage.org/jobs-and-labor/report/majority-union-members-now-work-the-government. April 2018.

Chapter NINE:

Engel Bromwich, Jonah. "Greenpeace Activists Arrested After Hanging 'Resist' Banner in View of White House." The New York Times, 25 January 2017. https://www.nytimes.com/2017/01/25/us/greenpeace-resist-banner-protest-trump.html. April 2018.

Mooney, Kevin. "This Health Care Nonprofit Gives Millions to Boost Obamacare and Far-Left Causes. What About the Public Interest?" The Daily Signal, 30 November 2015. https://www.dailysignal.com/2015/11/30/this-health-care-non-profit-gives-millions-to-boost-obamacare-and-far-left-causes-what-about-the-public-interest/. April 2018.

"20 Foundations and Trusts that fund LGBT programs." Funds for NGO's. https://www.fundsforngos.org/foundation-funds-for-ngos/20-foundations-trusts-fund-lgbt-programs/. April 2018.

"Tim Gill – Board Member." Gill Foundation. https://gillfoundation.org/board-member/tim-gill/. April 2018.

Linskey, Annie. "Elizabeth Warren's Native American problem goes beyond politics." Boston Globe, 19 January 2018. https://www.bostonglobe.com/news/nation/2018/01/19/elizabeth-warren-native-american-problem-goes-beyond-politics/uK9pGOl4JBmqmRUcxTNj3H/story.html. April 2018.

"Our Victories." Natural Resources Defense Council. https://www.nrdc.org/our-victories. April 2018.

Glabman, Maureen. "Health Plan Foundations: How Well Are They Spending the Money?" Managed Care, 1 August 2008. https://www.managedcaremag.com/archives/2008/8/health-plan-foundations-how-well-are-they-spending-money. April 2018.

Cawood, Jeffrey. "Health Foundation Helps Black Lives Matter Spread Anti-Cop Message." The Daily Wire. https://www.dailywire.com/news/25325/health-foundation-helps-black-lives-matter-spread-jeffrey-cawood.

Chung, André. "Has a Civil Rights Stalwart Lost Its Way?" Politico Magazine, July/August 2017. https://www.politico.com/magazine/story/2017/06/28/morris-dees-splc-trump-southern-poverty-law-center-215312. May 2018.

Chapter TEN:

"Organizing for America." Source Watch. https://www.sourcewatch.org/index.php/Organizing_for_America. April 2018.

Seitz-Wald, Alex. "Obama-Aligned Organizing for Action Relaunches for Trump Era." NBC News, 10 February 2017. https://www.nbcnews.com/storyline/democrats-vs-trump/obama-aligned-organizing-action-relaunches-trump-era-n719311. April 2018.

"Inside the Cave: An In-Depth Look at the Digital, Technology, and Analytics Operations of Obama for America." Engage Research. https://enga.ge/wp-content/uploads/2018/01/Inside_the_Cave-1.pdf. April 2018.

Chapter ELEVEN:

Snead, Jason. "Why Dissolving the Election Fraud Commission Is a True Loss for the Nation." The Daily Signal, 5 January 2018. https://www.dailysignal. com/2018/01/05/379558/. April 2018.

Preston, Bryan. "Massive Non-Citizen Voting Uncovered in Maryland." PJ Media, 29 October 2014. https://pjmedia.com/blog/massive-non-citizen-voting-un-covered-in-maryland/. April 2018.

Schmidt: Could Be 'Tens Of Thousands' Of Non-Citizens Who Registered To Vote In Pennsylvania." CBS News Philadelphia, 16 December 2017. http://phila-delphia.cbslocal.com/2017/12/16/schmidt-could-be-tens-of-thousands-of-non-citizens-who-registered-to-vote-in-pennsylvania/. April 2018.

Zimmerman, Malia. "Experts: California voter registration system 'highly susceptible' to fraud." Fox News Channel, 1 February 2017. http://www.foxnews. com/politics/2017/02/01/experts-california-voter-registration-system-high-ly-susceptible-to-fraud.html. April 2018.

Preston, Bryan. "Massive Non-Citizen Voting Uncovered in Maryland." PJ Media, 29 October 2014. https://pjmedia.com/blog/massive-non-citizen-voting-un-covered-in-maryland/. April 2018.

von Spakovsky, Hans. "Poll Shows Noncitizens Can Shape Elections." The Daily Signal, 2 June 2015. https://www.dailysignal.com/2015/06/02/poll-shows-noncit-izens-can-shape-elections/. April 2018.

Bedard, Paul. "Hillary drafts illegal 'Dreamers' to get immigrants to vote." Washington Examiner, 14 August 2016. https://www.washingtonexaminer.com/ hillary-drafts-illegal-dreamers-to-get-immigrants-to-vote/article/2599321. April 2018.

Mexican Man Charged With Using Fake ID, Voting in Elections." U.S. News, 26 October 2017. https://www.usnews.com/news/best-states/california/arti-cles/2017-10-26/mexican-man-charged-with-using-fake-id-voting-in-elections. April 2018.

Tyree, Elizabeth. "Student headed to prison for registering dead voters for Dem-ocrats." ABC News, 8 August 2017. http://wset.com/news/local/student-head-ed-to-prison-for-registering-dead-voters-for-democrats. April 2018.

Goldstein, David. "CBS2 Investigation Uncovers Votes Being Cast From Grave Year After Year." CBS Los Angeles, 23 May 2016. https://losangeles.cbslocal. com/2016/05/23/cbs2-investigation-uncovers-votes-being-cast-from-grave-year-after-year/. April 2018.

Snead, Jason. "Why Dissolving the Election Fraud Commission Is a True Loss for the Nation." The Daily Signal, 5 January 2018. https://www.dailysignal.

com/2018/01/05/379558/. April 2018.

Lucas, Fred. "Florida Democrat Election Official Admits Noncitizens, Felons Voting." The Daily Signal, 30 August 2017. https://www.dailysignal.com/2017/08/30/florida-democratic-election-official-admits-noncitizens-felons-voting/. April 2018.

"12 States (and DC) That Allow Driver's Licenses for People in the Country Illegally." ProCon.org, 3 February 2016. https://immigration.procon.org/view.resource.php?resourceID=005535. April 2018.

Chapter TWELVE:

Schwartz, Ian. "Maddow Exclusive: Trump 2005 Tax Return Shows He Paid $38 Million on $150 Million Income." RealClear Politics, 14 March 2017. https://www.realclearpolitics.com/video/2017/03/14/maddow_exclusive_trump_2005_tax_return_shows_he_paid_38_million_on_150_million_income.html. May 2018.

"Lemon Refuses to Report on Susan Rice Unmasking: We Won't 'Aid & Abet' a Diversion." Fox News, 4 April 2017. http://insider.foxnews.com/2017/04/04/don-lemon-cnn-susan-rice-unmasking-report-president-trump-wiretapping-claim. May 2018.

Savransky, Rebecca. "CNN's Chris Cuomo breaks down laughing when discussing Trump's marriage." The Hill, 26 February 2018. http://thehill.com/homenews/media/375582-cnns-chris-cuomo-breaks-down-laughing-when-discussing-state-of-trump-marriage. May 2018.

Nunez, Michael. "Former Facebook Workers: We Routinely Suppressed Conservative News." Gizmodo, 9 May 2016. https://gizmodo.com/former-facebook-workers-we-routinely-suppressed-conser-1775461006. May 2018.

"Facebook blocks Michael Savage for posting news on Islamic crime." WND, 1 August 2016. http://www.wnd.com/2016/08/facebook-blocks-michael-savage-for-migrant-murder-story/. May 2018.

Haverluck, Michael. "Censoring Christians: Google and Facebook and Twitter, oh my." NE News Now, 10 December 2017. https://onenewsnow.com/media/2017/12/10/censoring-christians-google-and-facebook-and-twitter-oh-my. May 2018.

Baklinski, Pete. "Youtube banned this powerful pro-life music video. Then the artist sued.." Life Site, 18 December 2015. https://www.lifesitenews.com/news/youtube-banned-this-powerful-pro-life-music-video.-then-the-artist-sued. May 2018.

Epstein, Robert. "The New Censorship." U.S. News, 22 June 2016. https://www.usnews.com/opinion/articles/2016-06-22/google-is-the-worlds-biggest-censor-and-its-power-must-be-regulated. May 2018.

Schaefer, Brett. "Ignore the critics: If Trump withdraws from Paris Climate Agreement, he will demonstrate US leadership." Fox News, 15 March 2017. http://www.foxnews.com/opinion/2017/03/15/ignore-critics-if-trump-with-draws-from-paris-climate-agreement-will-demonstrate-us-leadership.html. May 2018.

"Dennis Prager Sues 'Ideological' Google for Censoring Conservative YouTube Videos." Fox News, 6 March 2018. http://insider.foxnews.com/2018/03/06/den-nis-prager-lawsuit-against-google-youtube-restricting-conservative-videos. May 2018.

Bilger, Micaiah. "YouTube Censors Video Exposing Planned Parenthood's Abortion Agenda Hours After Its Release." LifeNews.com, 20 February 2018. http://www.lifenews.com/2018/02/20/youtube-censors-video-exposing-planned-par-enthoods-abortion-agenda-hours-after-its-release/. May 2018.

Nash, Charlie. "Twitter Unveils New 'Trust and Safety Council' Featuring Feminist Frequency." Breitbart, 9 February 2016. http://www.breitbart.com/tech/2016/02/09/twitter-unveils-new-trust-and-safety-council-featuring-fem-inist-frequency/. May 2018.

Neidig, Harper. "PragerU sues Google, YouTube for 'censoring' conserva-tive videos." The Hill, 24 October 2017. http://thehill.com/policy/technolo-gy/356966-prageru-sues-google-youtube-for-censoring-conservative-videos. May 2018.

De Young, Karen. "Under Trump, gains against ISIS have 'dramatically acceler-ated.'" The Washington Post, 4 August 2017. https://www.washingtonpost.com/world/national-security/under-trump-gains-against-isis-have-dramatically-ac-celerated/2017/08/04/8ad29d40-7958-11e7-8f39-eeb7d3a2d304_story.htm-l?noredirect=on&utm_term=.43f7cbda72c8. May 2018.

Stevenson, Peter. "Rachel Maddow's not-so-big reveal of Trump's tax returns [video]." The Washington Post, 15 March 2017. https://www.washingtonpost.com/video/politics/rachel-maddows-not-so-big-reveal-of-trumps-tax-re-turns/2017/03/15/35985290-099e-11e7-bd19-fd3afa0f7e2a_video.html?utm_ter-m=.8dff4dfdb33b. May 2018.

"At least 26 dead in Sutherland Springs, Texas church shooting; gunman identi-fied." ABC News, 5 November 2017. http://wjla.com/news/nation-world/multi-ple-injuries-reported-at-a-church-shooting-in-sutherland-springs-tex. May 2018.

Hanna, Jason et al. "Virginia governor to white nationalists: 'Go home ... shame on you.'" CNN, 13 August 2017. https://www.cnn.com/2017/08/12/us/charlottes-ville-white-nationalists-rally/index.html. May 2018.

Karimi, Faith and Holly Yan. "What's changed one month after the Parkland shooting." CNN, 14 March 2018. https://www.cnn.com/2018/03/14/us/parkland-school-shooting-a-month-later/index.html. May 2018.

Lee, Matthew. "Iran still top state sponsor of terrorism, U.S. report says." PBS, 19 July 2017. https://www.pbs.org/newshour/world/iran-still-top-state-sponsor-ter-rorism-u-s-report-says. May 2018.

Nash, Charlie. "Twitter Unveils New 'Trust and Safety Council' Featuring Feminist Frequency." Breitbart, February 9, 2016. http://www.breitbart.com/tech/2016/02/09/twitter-unveils-new-trust-and-safety-council-featuring-fem-inist-frequency/. May 2018.

"Trump in Israel Gave 'Rachashei Lev' Pediatric Cancer Patient Her Dream." The Yeshiva World, May 24, 2017. https://www.theyeshivaworld.com/news/israel-news/1284466/trump-israel-gave-rachashei-lev-pediatric-cancer-pa-tient-dream.html. June 2018.

"President Trump's Speech to the Arab Islamic American Summit." Whitehouse. gov, May 21 2017. https://www.whitehouse.gov/briefings-statements/presi-dent-trumps-speech-arab-islamic-american-summit/. June 2018.

Slefo, George. "Is Google in cahoots with Clinton campaign? Doubtful, but question persists." AdAge, 10 June 2016. http://adage.com/article/campaign-trail/google-cahoots-clinton-campaign/304442/. June 2018.

Chapter THIRTEEN:

"How the State Department is Undermining Trump's Agenda." American Great-ness, 21 October 2017. https://amgreatness.com/2017/10/21/how-the-state-de-partment-is-undermining-trumps-agenda/. June 2018.

King, Robert. "Little Sisters of the Poor battles states in court over birth control mandate." Washington Examiner, 21 November 2017. https://www.washington-examiner.com/little-sisters-of-the-poor-battles-states-in-court-over-birth-con-trol-mandate. June 2018.

Appelbaum, Binyamin. "What the Hobby Lobby Ruling Means for America." NY Times, 22 JULY 2014. https://www.nytimes.com/2014/07/27/magazine/what-the-hobby-lobby-ruling-means-for-america.html?mtrref=www.google.com&g-wh=4A8121B90AA43BB7BBBEE6C64BD5146E&gwt=pay. June 2018.

Sanders, Linley. "Who is Jack Phillips? Meet the Christian Baker in the Master-piece Cakeshop Supreme Court Case." Newsweek, 5 December 2017. http://www.newsweek.com/who-jack-phillips-meet-christian-baker-735094. June 2018.

Criss, Doug. "Judge rules California baker doesn't have to make wedding cake for same-sex couple." CNN, 8 February 2018. https://www.cnn.com/2018/02/08/us/wedding-cake-ruling-trnd/index.html. June 2018.

Paulson, Bob. "Washington Supreme Court Rules Against Barronelle Stutzman." Billy Graham Evangelistic Association, 28 April 2017. https://billygraham.org/decision-magazine/april-2017/washington-supreme-court-rules-barronelle-stutzman/. June 2018.

Cheves, John. "Appeals court says Hands On Originals did not discriminate against gays." Lexington Herald, 14 May 2017. http://www.kentucky.com/news/politics-government/article150169482.html. June 2018.

"Elane Photography v. Willock." Alliance Defending Freedom, 7 April 2014. http://www.adfmedia.org/news/prdetail/5537. June 2018.

Resmovits, Joy. "California's students will soon learn more LGBT history in schools." Los Angeles Times, 14 July 2016. http://www.latimes.com/local/lanow/la-me-lgbt-curriculum-california-20160714-snap-story.html. June 2018.

"Sex-change treatment for kids on the rise." CBS News, 20 February 2012. https://www.cbsnews.com/news/sex-change-treatment-for-kids-on-the-rise/. June 2018.

Hasson, Peter. "California Bill Forces Transgender Bathrooms Into Nursing Homes." The Daily Caller, 28 March 2017. http://dailycaller.com/2017/03/27/california-bill-forces-transgender-bathrooms-into-nursing-homes/. June 2018.

Starnes, Todd. "Bible Club shut down by Tennessee grade school." Fox News Opinion, 4 May 2017. http://www.foxnews.com/opinion/2017/05/04/bible-club-shut-down-by-tennessee-grade-school.html. June 2018.

Glessner, Thomas. "California Tried to Force Pro-Life Centers to Promote Abortion. Now, the Supreme Court Is Weighing In." The Daily Signal, 27 November 2017. https://www.dailysignal.com/2017/11/27/california-tried-to-force-pro-life-centers-to-promote-abortion-now-the-supreme-court-is-weighing-in/. June 2018.

Gjelten, Tom. "The Johnson Amendment in 5 Questions And Answers." NPR, 3 February 2017. https://www.npr.org/2017/02/03/513187940/the-johnson-amendment-in-five-questions-and-answers. June 2018.

Aizenman, Nurith. "Citing Abortions in China, Trump Cuts Funds for U.N. Family Planning Agency." NPR, 4 April 2017. https://www.npr.org/sections/goatsandsoda/2017/04/04/522040557/citing-abortions-in-china-trump-cuts-funds-for-u-n-family-planning-agency. June 2018.

Jones, Kevin. "Mexico City Policy ensures US funds won't force 'abortion ideology,' backers say." Catholic News Agency, 22 January 2018. https://www.catholicnewsagency.com/news/mexico-city-policy-ensures-us-funds-wont-force-abortion-ideology-backers-say-58991. June 2018.

LaBarbera, Peter. "Rainbow flag flies again at U.S. Embassy in Macedonia." Life Site, 19 May 2017. https://www.lifesitenews.com/news/rainbow-flag-flies-again-at-u.s.-embassy-in-macedonia. June 2018.

French, David. "How the Atlanta Fire Chief's Christian Views Cost Him His Job." National Review, 25 February 2016. https://www.nationalreview.com/2016/02/kelvin-cochran-christian-views-cost-atlanta-fire-chief-his-job/. June 2018.

Chapter FIFTEEN:

Evans, John. "The Pilgrims' Failed Experiment With Socialism Should Teach America A Lesson." Off The Grid News. https://www.offthegridnews.com/religion/the-pilgrims-failed-experiment-with-socialism-should-teach-america-a-lesson/. June 2018.

Sign up for Craig's FREE weekly newsletters.

Receive a free weekly newsletter in your email inbox filled with concise, need-to-know information, little-known trends and insider insights.

✓ The Huey Report (powerful insights on politics and economics) – Sign up today at
https://www.craighuey.com
Follow us on Facebook "@CraigAHuey" and on Twitter "@CraigHuey."

✓ Reality Alert (Christian worldview on key events and trends) – Sign up today at
https://www.electionforum.org
Follow us on Facebook "@realityalert" and on Twitter "@Reality_Alert."

✓ Direct Marketing Update (advanced direct response and digital advertising and marketing strategies and tactics) – Sign up today at
https://cdmginc.com
Follow us on Facebook "@cdmginc" and on Twitter "@CDMGINC."

☑ **Yes!** I want to discover how the Deep State is wielding a dangerous influence over government, culture and society — and what I can do to help stop it. Please send me my discounted copy of *The Deep State: 15 Surprising Dangers You Should Know* — plus my FREE special report on *"How Progressive Groups Are Fueling Deep State Resistance and Expansion."*

TWO PURCHASING OPTIONS (CHECK ONE):

☐ **Save 20%.** Send me 1 copy of *The Deep State: 15 Surprising Dangers You Should Know* – valued at $24.95 – for only $19.95, along with my FREE report, *"How Progressive Groups Are Fueling Deep State Resistance and Expansion."*

OR

☐ **Save Up to 30%.** Send me _____ copies of *The Deep State: 15 Surprising Dangers You Should Know* for only $16.95 per copy, along with my FREE report *"How Progressive Groups Are Fueling Deep State Resistance and Expansion."*

METHOD OF PAYMENT:

_____Check or money order made out to **Creative Direct Marketing Agency**

Charge my: _____VISA _____MasterCard _____American Express

Name (as it appears on card) _____

Card Number _____

Exp Date _____ 3-4 Digit Security Code_____

Signature _____

Street Address _____

City, State, ZIP _____

Email_____Phone #_____

Please sign me up for *The Huey Report* and *Reality Alert* –Craig's weekly newsletters on need-to-know news, shocking discoveries and insider insights for politics and economics (*The Huey Report*) and Evangelical Christians (*Reality Alert*).

MAIL THIS FORM TO:

Election Forum, 21171 S. Western Ave., Suite 260 Torrance, CA 90501
Or, visit www.deepstatebook.com to purchase a copy online today.